The Sunfood Cuisine

by Frédéric Patenaude
A Practical Guide to Raw Vegetarian Cuisine

The Sunfood Cuisine
by Frédéric Patenaude

This book contains little-known truths regarding the human body's amazing secrets.

A Note to the Reader:
Each lesson in this book contains facts, concepts, and ideas that build upon the lessons before it. Therefore, we recommend reading straight through and not skipping around the first time reading. The reading will surely prove most fruitful if you begin at the Table of Contents and read the chapters consecutively. It is our desire that a thousand years hence the contents of this book will be as up-to-date as at this moment. A lifestyle based on the cosmic laws is always in order and never becomes obsolete.

ISBN # 0-9653533-8-9
First Edition: November 1, 2001
Second Edition: June 1, 2003
Outside Cover Art: Sara Honeycutt
Inside Cover Art: Sara Honeycutt
Copyright 2001 Frédéric Patenaude

Printed on recycled paper by Genesis 129 Publishing
P.O. Box 900202, San Diego, CA 92190 U.S.A.
Call or write for a FREE catalog: 1-800-205-2350

DISCLAIMER

This book is sold with the understanding that the publisher, author, editor, and any related parties are not rendering professional services. The opinions, suggestions, and advice given in this book should not be viewed as medical advice.

The information contained in this book is subject to differences of opinion and interpretation. Every attempt was made to present accurate information as understood by the author.

Neither the publisher, author, editor, nor any involved or interested parties assume any liability for omissions or errors in this book, and therefore are not responsible for the interpretation or implementation of information contained in this book, and are not liable for any damages or loss caused, or alleged to be caused, directly, or indirectly, by information contained in this book, including, but not limited to, legal disputes.

The information in this book is not to be used as a substitute for the advice of a qualified health professional.

Each reader is encouraged to do their own research on issues that interest or concern them.

DEDICATION

This book is dedicated to **Nature's First Law**. It would not have happened without you. The author would also like to thank all the people who have contributed to this book, including the following:

Andrew Ethan Durham — For testing all my recipes, and being my friend.

Annie Jubb — For the inspiration.

Barbara Stead — For letting me stay at the Ranch.

Craig Lowellen "Emerald Spider"— For all I have learned from you during the WBF training, and after.

Dr. David Jubb — For all the teachings.

David Norman — For the pictures, and all the amazing help.

David Wolfe —For your constant support, knowledge, and inspiring dedication.

Dianne Onstad —For reading, re-reading, editing and getting this book ready for print.

Durian — For helping without asking anything in return.

Fred Silverbear — For patiently testing all my recipes back in January 2000!

J-C's Band — Pour avoir transformé l'amour spirituel en musique.

Jeremy Safron — For the raw chef skills.

John McCabe — For all the help, amazing insights, and sparkling ideas.

Liz — For testing some of the recipes, and for the support.

Louiselle — Merci pour m'avoir mis au monde.

Marianne Moineau — Pour avoir toujours cru en ce projet, et en moi.

Michael McCarthy — For the encouragement, insights, constant support, and for the raw yoga!

Morten Blakestone — For providing a roof at a time when I had little money, and nowhere to go.

Olivier Magnan — Merci pour toutes les sessions PNL et les conversations au téléphone. Longue vie à J.C.'s Band!

Raven Pelan — For encouraging me to finish this book. "You need to finish your book Fred, I need it!"

Réal Patenaude — Pour être mon père préféré!

Sara Honeycutt — For her inspiring conceptual art that graces the cover and pages of this book.

Sébastien Patenaude — Pour être mon frère, mon ami, et mon fan.

Sequoia Neptune — For the yoga!

Stephen Arlin — For the time at NFL, the laughs, and all the help.

Suzie Bohannon — For the raw chef skills.

FOREWORD

There is an old riddle that asks, "Who did <u>not</u> discover water?" The answer is, of course, a fish. The reason why a fish could never discover water is because water is too obvious to a fish. In the same manner of this riddle, some truths go unseen because they are so obvious.

Many people wonder what is humanity's ideal food. Trillions of dollars have been spent studying the issue. What the studies have concluded is very obvious: raw plants.

Just like the air we breathe and the water we drink, raw plants have always surrounded us, and have always been the staple of human diets. Evidence of raw fruits, vegetables, nuts and seeds have been found in the food preparation areas of ancient ruins throughout the world. And, despite some predictions that humans would be eating nothing but manufactured food items by the 21st century, plants remain the most natural and healthiest food choice.

Plants are convenient foods. Unlike animals, plants do not scurry away when we try to gather them for our consumption. Plants provide us with the variety of nutrients our bodies need to grow and stay healthy and, as with an apple, they are a convenient size for us to eat.

The focus of this book is on uncooked — or "raw" — foods consisting of vegetables, fruits, seeds and nuts. Another term for "raw plant food" is "Sunfood." The term Sunfood has a noble quality that implies food grown under the sun, and means food that is truly raw and natural. Sunfood has the most important ingredient of all: positive life-force energy. In a world overwhelmed with death, pain, fire and destruction, Sunfoods provide hope for a more joyful life and rejuvenation of being at all levels.

Sunfood makes us feel alive and fresh. People have always been drawn toward plants to beautify and enliven their surroundings. Their vibrant energies enliven us, and we are naturally attracted to their smells and colors. Even when humans create artificial scents, as in perfumes or cleansers, they create fragrances similar to those of flowers and plants. When you ask a child to name their favorite scents, they are likely to mention flowers or berries; it is highly unlikely that they will mention cheese or beef. Similarly, there are no cheese-scented soaps, or beef-scented shampoos. Soaps and shampoos are scented after fruits and flowers because the beauty and vibrancy of those plants are most desirable to us.

What is most important in selecting the type of food to eat is that you choose what is natural and nutritious for the body. Foods that are unprocessed and uncooked contain all of their original vitamins, colloidal minerals, enzymes and trace nutrients. Uncooked fruits, vegetables, nuts and seeds are the most natural foods.

Enzymes are a key element found in raw foods which are absent in cooked foods, because heating destroys enzymes. This is one of the reasons why cooked food is not the best thing to put into the body. Food enzymes are required for proper digestion, and if they are not present in the food itself, must be secreted by the pancreas. An excessive intake of cooked food over a lifetime will cause the pancreas to swell and malfunction.

Uncooked natural plant food also contains another vital element: electrified water. The first thing that dissipates during cooking is electrified water. Having been raised by two parents who are medical doctors, and seeing their patients over the years, I have clearly noticed that illness and aging seem to correspond with chronic dehydration caused by eating cooked food. This phenomena has been confirmed by my friend and colleague, Dr. Gabriel Cousens, who describes that a healthy body is more than 80% water, but with age and illness that can decrease to 60%. This is one reason why it is important to get high-quality water in the daily diet, such as the water that is contained in uncooked plant substances.

"You are what you eat" is a profound and cosmic truth. It is written into the fabric of the universe. During my years of travelling and lecturing on health and nutrition, I have found this saying to be the only phrase that absolutely everybody knows! We know that if we eat incredible food, we feel incredible. Adopting a Sunfood Lifestyle (which means eating raw plant foods at the level that is most appropriate for us) enhances the overall quality of life. Eating raw plant food is the key life-giving enhancer that makes everything else work better.

When people ask me how to transition into a Sunfood Lifestyle, I always respond that this whole lifestyle is about adding foods in, not taking any foods away. When one adds Sunfoods over a period of time, and learns what are healthy choices for the body to function optimally, improper foods become less desirable, both because the body and the person are ready to let go of them. This book is valuable because it provides information that makes adding Sunfoods into your life a fun and exciting, yet sensible, adventure.

This "uncookbook" is designed as a companion guide to my book **The Sunfood Diet Success System**. As you read that book, refer back to these pages often to give yourself more knowledge on how to create tastier treats and more nourishing meals for your friends and family.

Having worked closely with Frédéric Patenaude, I know that his skills and knowledge in this field are unsurpassed. Frédéric and I worked together studying and distributing hundreds of books on the subject of raw-veganism. His commitment to creating the greatest cuisine shines through in every wonderful recipe. Frédéric has artistically created countless gourmet Sunfood meals for guests at my health lectures and retreats all over the world. His recipes taste great, are easy to make, and are thoroughly satisfying. Enjoy!

David Wolfe (**www.davidwolfe.com, www.thebestdayever.com**), Author of **The Sunfood Diet Success System** and **Eating For Beauty**, Publisher of **The Sunfood Cuisine**, Founder of the non-profit Fruit Tree Planting Foundation (**www.fruittreefoundation.org**), and co-founder of **www.rawfood.com**

Introduction

"The sun is the source of all life on this planet." This is a powerful concept we all know and, to some degree, one that is part of all mythologies. For as long as humans have existed, they have been aware of the power of the sun. It is what makes plants grow and without it, no life would be possible on this planet. When the sun shines, everyone feels better, for the light of the sun is indispensable in keeping our bodies and spirits alive and alight.

Sunfoods are plant-based foods that contain the life-force of the sun. Sunfoods are the beautiful fruits, vegetables and nuts that have been grown in the sun, without the use of chemical fertilizers and pesticides. They carry within them all the radiant life-giving energy of the sun. They are alive because they have not been prepared using fire, heating, or cooking. Foods that have been cooked and denatured no longer carry that life-force.

This book is called **The Sunfood Cuisine**, because I use ingredients that still carry the sun's energy; in other words, foods that have not been cooked. Throughout this book you will learn a completely different approach to making foods. Instead of thinking in terms of frying, boiling, and roasting, you will be learning how to combine the intense flavors of fruits, vegetables, nuts, herbs and spices, to create tasty and healthy meals.

It is wonderful when, after a meal, you no longer need to scrub the grease off of your pots and pans. In fact, what the cooked foods do to your pots and pans is a testament to what they do in your body. The greasy and starchy foods often ferment inside of you, sticking to the walls of your intestines and clogging your system. On the other hand, clean foods leave clean dishes. And they leave you clean on the inside!

Eating an abundance of raw fruits and vegetables is one of the single most important things you can do to improve your health, your life, and your appearance. You will learn in this book about some of the marvelous properties of raw fruits and vegetables which, I am sure, will encourage you to include a large portion of these foods in your diet.

The recipes in this book are tasty and easy to prepare. To prepare them, you will only need a few basic pieces of kitchen equipment. But if all you have is a knife, a cutting board and a bowl, you will still be able to prepare most of the recipes.

This book has been written as an intended companion to David Wolfe's book entitled **The Sunfood Diet Success System**. The title of this book is actually derived from David Wolfe's book. Those needing inspiration and a greater understanding of the raw-vegan diet will likely find what they are looking for in David Wolfe's book, as well as the companion website for this book, **www.rawvegan.com**, and David Wolfe's website, **www.davidwolfe.com**.

Thank you for reading **The Sunfood Cuisine**. It has been a pleasure to write, and it is an even greater pleasure to see people benefiting from it. I have put all of the love I could into the creation of the recipes, and if you put as much love into their preparation, you will be eating the most alive meals on the planet.

Frédéric Patenaude
April, 2003

Author, Raw Food Chef Frédéric Patenaude

PART 1: THE SUNFOOD DIET

CHAPTER 1: WHY SUNFOODS?

Many people throughout the world want to move away from their traditional diets of processed grains and animal products and towards a healthier diet. Research shows that the consumption of raw fruits and vegetables is one of the basic keys to good health. Many people know that raw fruits and vegetables are healthy foods and strive to eat them everyday. However, few realize that raw fruits and vegetables are so important that they should be your primary foods. This book will help you move away from the typical cooked, denatured and processed foods, and enter into the realm of raw and living foods — which I refer to as "Sunfoods."

There are many reasons why you should be eating mostly raw and living foods. Most of these reasons come from scientific research, and some of them from common sense — as well as the personal experience of millions of people throughout the world who have experienced the benefits of eating raw fruits and vegetables as the base of their diet.

IT MAKES SENSE

First, eating raw foods makes sense. Think about it. All creatures living on this planet thrive on a natural diet of raw plant foods. Humans are the only creatures cooking their food. Many have seen this as a great achievement, following the old belief that raw foods are hard to digest, and that cooking somehow improves their digestibility. Many scientists attribute all the greatest accomplishments of humanity to cooking and agriculture. But if this were true, then why are humans the sickest creatures on the planet? We are not thriving like wild animals are. Wild animals, living on raw foods, have an amazing vitality that enables them to survive the harshest living conditions. Could you imagine what would happen if a tribe of wild wolves started feeding on donuts and cooked meat? Do you think they would continue to thrive? Far from it. No creature can thrive on devitalized foods, and humans are no exception.

Eating raw foods makes sense because we are naturally attracted to these foods. Imagine for a second that you have been left on a desert island with no tools or technology. Now it's time to eat. What do you do? What are you naturally inclined to do? Start chasing a wild animal, catch it with your bare hands, and eat it alive? Find a cow and hope to be able to steal its milk? Graze? Catch a fish and eat it raw? Or maybe pick fruits and berries from the bushes and trees? Which option is the most appealing? I bet that the fruit option is. Why? Because this is what you are naturally attracted to. Humans are meant to eat raw fruits and vegetables — this is our natural diet.

Harvey Diamond, author of the wonderful book **Fit for Life**, which inspired so many people to eat their fruits and vegetables, used to say: "Give a baby a banana and a live rabbit. I can bet you my car that every single time the baby will eat the banana and play with the rabbit." The contrary would be quite a disturbing sight. Why do we feel it should be that way? Because this is how humans are meant to live.

Human babies have purer instincts than human adults, and are attracted to fruit. Why is it that many of the most popular foods made for children and babies are "fruit flavored," or shaped like fruit? Babies and children are naturally attracted to fruit, especially tropical fruits such as mangos and papayas. Children have to learn to enjoy the taste of meat and potatoes, but they naturally enjoy the taste of mangos, bananas, and papayas.

Eating raw fruits and vegetables makes sense because this is what we are supposed to eat. As you start eating more of these foods, you will likely realize that *this is the most natural and normal way to eat and live.*

ENZYMES AND LIFE-FORCE
Enzymes are often thought of as the life-force in foods. Enzymes are what make a green fruit ripen and become sweet and delicious. Enzymes make it possible for a seed to sprout and grow into a plant. They are also the digestive forces that our bodies need in order to break the food into the nutrients that are assimilable by the cells. Without enzymes, no life would be possible on this planet. This is why enzymes are said to be the "catalysts" of life.

Whenever you heat or cook food over 110 degrees Fahrenheit (43 degrees Celsius), the enzymes in the food start to die. After a few seconds of being exposed to high temperatures, all enzymes in food become dead. How can you demonstrate that? Take two seeds. Bake one at 350 degrees for 2 minutes, do nothing with the other one. Now plant the two seeds and water them. Which one will never grow? The cooked seed. Why? Because all of the enzymes were destroyed by heat, and what is left is a dead seed that can no longer sprout.

A lot of research completed by Dr. Edward Howell and other scientists show that the enzymes in food are needed to properly digest food. If they are not present—as when they have been destroyed by cooking—the body has to supply its own enzymes, which eventually depletes its supplies, leading to physical degeneration and disease.

Besides enzymes, there seems to be a more powerful factor involved in eating raw and living foods. We call this the "life-force factor." We differentiate this from the enzyme factor because we believe life-force to be more fundamental

Plants, like animals, possess a life-force. It is what makes them grow, thrive, and become beautiful. When we eat plants, we absorb their life-force. The life-force of the plant is transferred to us and becomes part of us.

When we cook plants we kill their life-force. When we eat cooked food we eat food that is dead and lifeless. Think about the difference between a raw carrot and a cooked carrot. The raw carrot is strong, colorful, and alive. You could plant it and it would probably grow. What about the cooked carrot? It is limp, less colorful, and life-less. Its fresh taste is gone, and its appearance is not as vibrant.

The life-force factor of raw and living food is not something scientific. I do not mention this as a scientific argument, but only because science has not found a method to accurately measure the life-force in food. If we could measure the life-force in food with a scientific method, we would quickly recognize how raw plant foods are full of life-force, and how cooked foods are devoid of the same life-force.

There is one method, though, that exists to measure the life-force of things. It is called "Kirlian Photography." The Kirlian camera is a special type of camera that can capture the life-force, or aura, of plants and animals. It can also capture the energy emanating from crystals. Kirlian photographs blatantly show how cooked foods are devoid of life-force, and how raw and living foods are full of life-force. Photographs in David Wolfe's book **Eating For Beauty** show the difference between raw cabbage and cooked cabbage. The raw cabbage literally glows with color and vitality. The cooked cabbage, in comparison, is dark and life-less, with few colors. We have included Kirlian photos in this book (page 29), showing the difference between the auric field of the hands of a person who consumes junk food, and a person who consumes healthy foods. The difference in the fields of energy that are emanating from these two people's hands, and that are picked up by the camera is quite staggering. Surrounding the first person's hands we can barely see any energy. Around the second person, the one who lives on healthy foods, we can see energetic patterns of all kinds.

The life-force is the most important factor in food. It is not a scientific factor, but it is one that you can easily recognize as true. It appeals to common sense, and you probably have been able to see examples in your own life. Just try this for yourself. See how you feel after you eat uncooked, living fruits and vegetables, and how you feel in comparison when you eat dead foods, such as meat and cooked potatoes. The difference of life-force in your body should be enough to convince you of the benefits of raw fruits and vegetables.

COOKING DESTROYS THE PATTERNS OF NATURE

Nature forms everything in patterns. There are patterns within the roots, trunks, stems, and branches of trees and plants. Patterns are also in the forms and colors of the leaves, flowers, fruits, and vegetables. On a smaller scale, there are patterns in the way the cells of the plants are arranged, and within the cells there are patterns in the DNA, and in the molecules. Nature also creates patterns in animals and humans. There are basic symmetrical patterns in the way the feet, legs, arms, and hands are formed. And there is symmetry in the features of the torso, face, and internal organs. The patterns formed by nature are seen throughout the body, including in the cells, DNA, and molecules.

What the act of cooking does is destroy what Nature has formed on a molecular level. Those who eat a raw-vegan diet are eating food the way Nature created it, with all of its nutrients and intricate molecular patterns undamaged by heat. They are putting natural patterns into their body, which the body uses to create itself on a molecular level, and in a pattern that only Nature can create. Those who eat a cooked diet, whether it be a vegan, vegetarian or carnivorous diet, are putting into their mouths food which is no longer what Nature created, but that which is unnatural. Because of this, the cooked food eaters are likely to experience health conditions that are not seen in those who follow a natural, well-rounded, raw-vegan diet.

Science has shown over and over again that those who eat an unhealthy diet lacking in fresh fruits and vegetables are not as healthy as those who do. Those who eat certain types of cooked and unnatural foods experience certain types of health problems. Those who eat a lot of meat and animal products are likely to experience heart problems, and certain types of cancers. Those who eat diets lacking in certain nutrients are likely to experience certain health problems related to inadequate nutrition. But those who eat a well-rounded raw-vegan diet are much less likely to experience the health problems that are seen in the populations of people who follow cooked-food diets. Also, those who follow cooked-food diets are more likely to lack certain nutrients. This is because cooking destroys many nutrients. Eating raw-vegan foods provides better nutrition because the nutrients, including vitamins, minerals, amino acids, enzymes, and trace elements have not been destroyed or harmed by cooking.

WATER-RICH FOODS

Water is a critically important factor for good health. Many people understand the importance of drinking enough water, but few are able to live up to the recommendations given by doctors, which is to drink 8 to 10 large glasses of water every day.

Drinking plenty of water is important for many reasons. One is because water is largely what we are composed of, and it is constantly evaporating through our skin. Water is Nature's preferred solvent, and is used by the body to flush out toxins produced by the cells. If you do not take in enough water, you will experience symptoms associated with intoxication, such as headaches and constipation. Water is needed for the transportation of certain water-soluble nutrients. Also, the good bacteria that live in the intestines need water to survive.

One problem that most people have is that their food is largely devoid of living water. Everything you eat has to be turned into a liquid before your body can assimilate the nutrients within it. When you put a piece of bread into your mouth, your body has to use an incredible amount of energy to break it down, and rarely succeeds entirely in doing so. But when you eat a piece of fruit, such as a papaya which is mostly water, your body digests it with ease.

Water-rich foods are important because they keep the body clean. They are digested quickly, and the water in them helps to flush toxins out of the system. If you do not eat many water-rich foods, you will have to drink a lot of water to compensate. But the water that most people drink is quite toxic. Water coming out of a tap, and even some bottled water, is polluted with heavy metals and inorganic minerals. Also, water kept in plastic bottles contains gasses that leach out of the plastic.

The best and highest quality water can be found in fresh, organically grown fruits and vegetables. The water found in fruits and vegetables is pure because the plant itself through its roots has filtered it. There is no other source of water that matches the quality of water found in organically grown and wild plants.

Your body will function more regularly in the elimination department when fueled with the high-quality water found in organically grown fruits and vegetables. Cooked and dead foods have a tendency to clog the body. Raw fruits and vegetables do the opposite, and keep your system clean and running smoothly.

TOXINS IN COOKED FOOD

Cooked foods are the product of complex chemical reactions that even science has a difficult time understanding. Think about it: with a few basic pieces of equipment—a stove and a few pots and pans—you can radically transform your food, play with it, and transform its chemical composition on a molecular level. Think about the difference between a raw potato, and a potato after it has been baked. What a metamorphosis! And all of this you could not have achieved without this little magical feat you performed using the flames of your stove. But what is it that really goes on behind the scenes when we cook our foods? What is it that happens at the molecular level that can turn this raw potato into the food we know as a "baked potato?"

Cooking has always been considered an "art." Every possible way of transforming food has been permitted, as long as it was successful in creating something pleasing to the palate. This so-called art had the benefit of being able to use the rich, natural world to operate its marvels. It is possible, using the molecules contained in foods and transforming them using fire, to create countless new molecules that were not naturally present in the original foods. These new molecules are the true offspring of cooking, and their possible impact on human health is quite scary. Science is just starting to analyze these new creations of the cooking art, and because of the gigantic number of chemicals created by heat, there is no end in sight.

Rarely are chefs interested in the complexities of science, and it might scare them to think of their art as cold science. But the amazing laws of science only ask us to admit that our Universe is composed of molecules, which are in themselves composed of atoms. Living things are made up of patterns of cells, which are made up of patterns of molecules. Most of us have known this since grade school. We also know that atoms are linked together by chemical reactions that are stronger or weaker according to their type: between the atoms of a same molecule, the forces are generally strong, but between two different neighboring molecules the forces of attraction are weaker.

Often when we heat something, we break only the forces playing against the neighboring molecules. Turning water into ice is an example of stacking water molecules. When we heat ice, the energy that we bring suffices to break the links between the water molecules, and thus creates a liquid where the molecules, although forming a coherent mass, are moving from one another. However, in the liquid form, the molecules are not transformed, as the molecules of water are identical to the molecules of ice. Then again, when we heat water over 212 degrees (100 Celsius), it evaporates, because the heat that has been added is enough to break the forces of cohesion between the water molecules. Yet within each molecule the atom of oxygen is still linked to two atoms of hydrogen. This type of transformation is physical in its nature and not chemical: the water molecule stays a water molecule.

But, what the average chef does not know is that chemical reactions occur during the cooking process. This is because molecules in foods are being disassociated, rearranged, and new molecules are being created.

Here is what Guy Claude Burger wrote about one of the scientists working with the chemical changes in cooked foods (from **Manger Vrai**):

> "In 1916, an American chemical engineer by the name of Maillard decided to isolate substances that give cooked foods their distinctive flavors, such as the tastes of bread, chocolate, and coffee. After having singled them out, he hoped, no doubt, to produce them artificially in order to add them to industrial foods and enhance the appeal that they could have to the consumer's taste buds. So, in order to complete his scheme, he had to determine the exact structure of these new molecules. He quickly found that these molecules resulted from very complex, haphazard chemical reactions between sugars and proteins, and one could produce them quite easily by heating any food even to moderate temperatures.
>
> It is not possible to see with the naked eye what happens in a saucepan on the molecular level. When a chemist combines two substances in a test tube, and subsequently heats the compound over a Bunsen burner, it boils, clouds, changes color, or explodes accordingly. In each case, a new compound has been produced. Heat causes the molecules involved to collide, and repeated collision causes deviant bonding in order for new molecules, and hence a new substance, to form. The same goes for cooking, except that myriad molecules are brought together instead of just two.
>
> In an ordinary baked potato, there are already 450 by products of every description. They have even been named 'new chemical composites.' So far, around 50 such substances were studied and turned out to be either peroxiding, anti-oxidizing, or toxic, and possibly even mutagenic, meaning that they are liable to wreck cell nuclei and set up cancer. What was ascertained for broiled potatoes, which involves a fairly straightforward preparation, becomes much more serious with more sophisticated cookery. Sliced potatoes baked with cheese is a case in point. Heating releases an awesome array of chemical reactions—450 substances in potatoes, and probably many more in cheese, which is a highly intricate biochemical complex. Not only will those unwanted molecules stack up their effects, but, moreover, they will combine among themselves in every possible way—meaning that tens of thousands of abnormal substances will spring out of a cooked dish calling for mere potatoes and cheese. Just think of elaborate recipes where one clocks up endless chains of sundry ingredients jumbled together helter-skelter."

It seems that shortly after Maillard discovered these molecules—that have since been termed "Maillard's molecules"—he tried to prove that they had no adverse effect on human health. Some experiments quickly showed that he was wrong, and all his work was swept under the rug—until 1982, when some of his research appeared in scientific journals. Scientists are now beginning to see the connection between the introduction of these molecules into human bodies and common health problems.

From *Pyrolysis and Risks of Toxicity* by Professor R. Derache in "Cahiers de nutrition et de diztique" (Diet and nutrition Journal), 1982, p. 39:

> "As far back as 1916, Maillard proved that the brown pigments and polymers that occur in pyrolysis (chemical breakdown by heat alone)... are yielded after prior reaction of an amino acid group with the carbonyl group of sugars.
>
> Though apparently simple, this reaction is, in fact, highly complex, itinerating in a spate of successive reactions and forming melanoidins, which are brown pigments that impart a typical color to whatever part of a food has endured higher temperatures.
>
> The number of substances generated as a result is most impressive, yielding endless chains of new molecules: ketones, esters, aldehydes, ethers, volatile alcohols, and non-volatile heterocycles, etc. These innumerable substances coalesce into a complex compound, and are endowed with differing biological and chemical attributes: they are toxic, aromatic, peroxiding, anti-oxidizing, and possibly mutagenic and carcinogenic (DNA fractures can be oncogenic), or even anti-mutagenic and anti-carcinogenic. This to say that heating causes widespread disruption in the natural order of molecules."

The research backing this article evidenced over 50 pyrolytic substances in broiled potatoes alone, most of which originated from pyroseines and thiazole. However, Derache also states that "there remain, all in all, some 400 by-products to identify."

The brown color that chefs try to obtain while sautéing foods in oil is a color created through the Maillard reaction. The reaction occurs when high temperatures are reached by the fat content in food. It occurs less often when we boil foods because temperatures there are limited to the temperature of boiling water (212 degrees Fahrenheit, or 100 degrees Celsius).

The Maillard reaction is one type of possible reaction occurring during common food preparation, but not the only one. Cooked foods are the product of chemical reactions, and most transformations operated by the culinary art are chemical in their nature. When meat darkens on the surface as it is cooked, this is the result of a chemical reaction; when brown rice softens when boiled, this is also a chemical reaction. Unlike water, the molecules in food are extremely complex and fragile, leaving places for a huge amount of new chemistry in the cooking pan.

Cooking food is more than just one reaction - it is a mass of innumerable complex reactions that we simplify using the classifications of biochemists: carbohydrates, fats, proteins, water and minerals. The products of these reactions are innumerable, and still mostly unknown.

There are multiple reasons to believe that new molecules created during the process of cooking enter the blood stream without being properly digested, since there are no enzymes adapted for their digestion. These molecules would then accumulate in all parts of the body to create any number of conditions that we commonly refer to as diseases.

Many researchers think that there is no reason for the body to be adapted to the new molecules created in the process of cooking due to their huge quantities and complexity, and the fact that they have entered human bodies only in the past 10,000 years of human history.

The Maillard reaction works simultaneously upon thousands of compounds with innumerable combinations. When we cook food, we create molecules of unknown consequence to human health. So it is not hard to see how some of these molecules, in minimal concentration, could be at the origin of many serious health problems.

VITAMINS, MINERALS AND ANTIOXIDANTS
Raw fruits and vegetables are filled with vitamins and minerals which cooked and denatured foods lack because many nutrients are damaged and destroyed during the cooking process.

It is quite obvious that cooking destroys the nutritional quality of food since heating is a destructive process in itself. When you apply fire to something, it becomes less than it was. When you apply fire to your food, it becomes less than it was. You cannot "add" to your food by cooking it. You can only "subtract" from it, or alter it. When you fry vegetables, do they become more or less than they were before? They become less. They lose some of their nutritional value because fire destroys and does not create. Try putting your finger into the boiling water next time you make pasta (not for too long!), and you will realize what I mean by this "destructive process" we refer to as "cooking." Your finger will get burned if you leave it in the boiling water. Your food is also burned and damaged when you boil or heat it in any way…cooking kills your food, metaphorically speaking!

Many nutrients are lost during the cooking process. Some foods that most people eat nearly every day are devoid of nutrients. For example, white bread

DIRTY ARTERIES

Your intestines are not the only part of your body that gets obstructed on a typical cooked food diet. Your arteries also get clogged. At the time of this writing, heart-related disease remains the most prevalent cause of death in North America and Europe. Clogged arteries are killing people on these continents by the millions every year.

All the research on heart disease seems to point to the following: diet is strongly linked to heart disease, and the best way to improve your diet is to reduce your intake of meat and other saturated fat-containing foods, while increasing your consumption of fresh fruits and vegetables.

It has been demonstrated that saturated fat triggers the bad cholesterol in your body to rise, which leads to clogged arteries and eventually heart disease. But not all types of fat are bad for you. The fat found in avocados, olives, flax seeds, hemp seeds, and other nuts and seeds have been shown to reduce the amount of bad cholesterol. This is one of the reasons why people living in the Mediterranean regions, while eating a diet high in fat, have a low incidence of heart disease compared to Americans. This is because most of the fat they eat comes from cold-pressed olive oil, and other plant sources.

Fat found in meat, on the other hand, has been shown to cause heart disease and clogged arteries. Many people experience a significant reduction in their cholesterol level just by becoming vegetarian. Nations that are the heaviest meat eaters, such as United States and Canada, have the highest incidence of heart disease. Researchers have also found that certain components in raw fruits and vegetables help to keep the arteries clean; thus, raw plant foods not only do not cause heart disease in the first place, but can help reverse the condition by cleaning the arteries.

CANCER

Another common cause of pain and death in industrialized societies is cancer. About one quarter of the population in North America is affected by cancer at some point or another, and many die from it. Although scientists have promised many cures since U.S. President Richard Nixon declared a "war on cancer" over thirty years ago, none of the research has led anywhere. More people are dying of cancer every year in the U.S. than died of it thirty years ago. It has been found that cancer is strongly related to diet and lifestyle. Everyone knows that smoking causes lung cancer, but few are willing to admit that steak causes colon cancer, even though there is enough research to prove it.

On the other hand, it is in raw fruits and vegetables that we find the highest concentration of cancer-fighting components, such as antioxidants like vitamin C. Many studies have shown that diets that include plenty of raw fruits and vegetables are associated with a lower risk of cancer.

By eating a diet consisting of raw plant foods, you are lowering your chances of getting cancer in two ways. First, you are not ingesting most of the food substances that cause it; and second, you are eating the foods that help to prevent it.

BIOLOGICAL ADAPTATION

I have a belief, and I cannot tell you if it is true. I just know it to be true. This belief tells me that Nature did not make a mistake when She created life on this planet. Nature provided food for all of Her creatures, and I believe that She provided food for us too. All the creatures on this planet seem to find foods in their environment without needing to transform it in any way. All creatures on this planet have a natural diet, which they live on, and I believe that humans are no exception. I believe that we can find everything we need to eat right from the trees and the plants, without needing to transform or alter it in any way. When we cook foods because we think cooking makes them more digestible, it is like saying that Nature made a mistake when presenting us with the foods in their natural state. Wouldn't it make more sense if we ate food in the form Nature created it for us, and not feel compelled to transform it from its natural state?

Our natural foods are raw fruits and vegetables. These are the foods we are attracted to in their natural state. We enjoy eating fruits on their own, munching on lettuce and celery, and also snacking on raw nuts and seeds. But who likes to shove raw meat down their throat, or take a handful of raw grains and eat them? Nobody does (or almost nobody), because these foods do not taste great in their natural state. We have to cook them in order to enjoy them. And I believe that Nature gave us the senses of taste and smell so we could determine what is good to eat and what is not. Ideally, I would say that if it does not taste good in its raw, natural state, then maybe you should not be eating it.

Do not take my word for everything that I have said in this chapter. Try it for yourself. I cannot convince you of anything. I did not write this book to sell you a belief. Your own intuition and judgement will tell you what is right for you, which may not be the same as what is right for me, or for your neighbor. But let me ask you to do something: just try it! Try living on nothing but raw fruits and vegetables, eating them in abundance, and see what happens to both your physical and mental states. Eat at least 80% raw fruits and vegetables, using the recipes in this book, for the next two weeks and see how you feel. Then go back to eating less than 10% raw fruits and vegetables, and compare the difference. Anyone can do something for two weeks, especially if there is a possibility it may change his or her life in a great way.

You will inevitably find, when you eat more fruits and vegetables, you feel better. And that the heavy meals of meat, milk, and cooked starches sap your energy and vitality.

This is the power of Sunfood: fruits and vegetables contain vitality from the sun. When you eat alive, you feel alive!

An electromagnetic Kirlian photo of a watermelon
(photo by Christopher Wodtke, www.kirlian.com)

*Kirlian photo of the hands of
a person eating a living-food diet.*

*Kirlian photo of the hands of
a person eating a junk-food diet.*

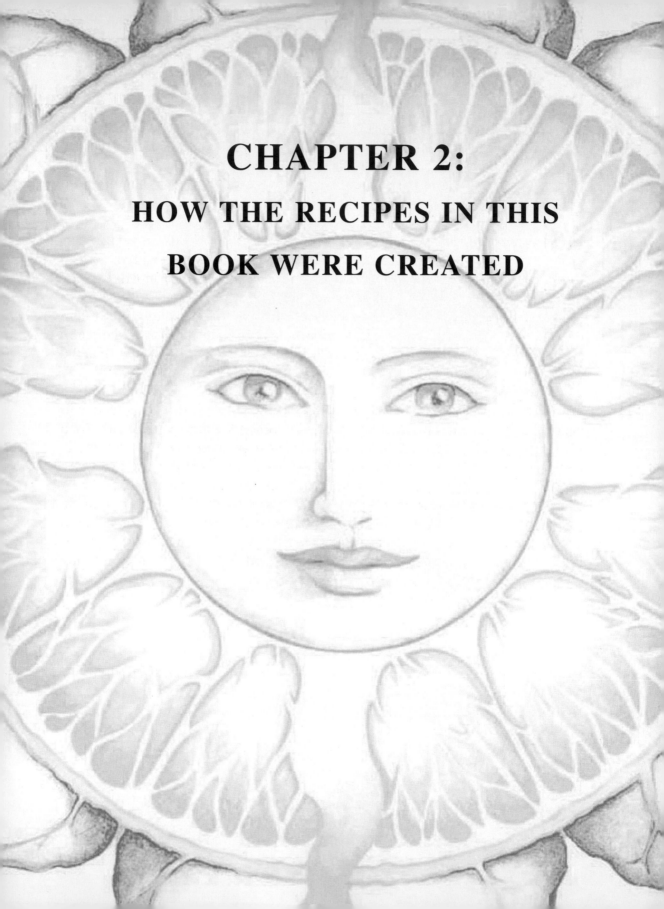

CHAPTER 2:

HOW THE RECIPES IN THIS
BOOK WERE CREATED

Food has to taste good. When switching to a diet of healthy, life-enriching foods, your food should taste better. Most health recipe books today provide you with incredibly tasteless and bland recipes. But the whole point of making recipes is to add flavor and nutrition to your life. When I prepare a meal, I want it to taste as good as possible. My motto is this: your meals should look and taste better than cooked food. This is why the recipes in this book have been created to be pleasing to the palate. I wanted every single one of them to be an explosion of pleasure in your mouth.

In my opinion, we should be eating 95-100% raw plant foods, mostly unseasoned and unmixed. We have been raised eating a lot of savory and rich cooked foods, so going back to a simple diet is too much of a gap for most people. I have created the recipes in this book so that you can eat healthy by incorporating more fruits, vegetables, nuts and seeds into your diet without sacrificing the pleasure of eating. As you will soon become aware, it is possible to be really creative with raw foods by making meals that will look and taste better than the foods you are probably used to.

To make super-tasty foods, I choose to use some condiments that you will become familiar with in a short while. It is important to have fun with your food and enjoy it. Many people have an approach to diet that is too restrictive. Because of this, many of these people become obsessed with diet and food, and sometimes eat very large quantities of food in order to compensate for their frustration. They rarely succeed in the long term, and often become irrational in their food choices. That is why I think it is important to be able to prepare meals that you will truly enjoy, without any frustration. Sure there will be some sacrifices required on your part, but those sacrifices will be well compensated for by all the new delicious foods that you will learn to enjoy, and in the long term by greatly improved health.

If you feel that some of the condiments I use do not suit you, simply leave them out or substitute another. Remember that you are not obliged to use them if you feel like eating in a simpler way. The main ingredients in the book are the fruits and vegetables, so you will still be able to enjoy the recipe ideas, no matter how you choose to eat.

The recipes in this book were created between 1998 and 2000 as I travelled through North America educating myself on the subject of vegetarianism, rawfoodism, and health. I stayed with numerous Sunfoodists (people eating a high percentage of raw plant foods), and worked at different restaurants and retreat centers. Wherever I went, people would always be impressed by the food I made. I would pull out whatever was in the refrigerator, make a meal out of it, and often they would say: "This might just be the best soup (or salad) I ever had!" Most of these recipes are transcripts of meals that have been made on the spot, with whatever was available in the refrigerator wherever I happened to be staying. Many where thrown together in less than ten minutes, and were written down because everyone was telling me, "This is so good Frédéric! You have to write down this recipe!"

Understand that healthy cuisine is fun! And **The Sunfood Cuisine** is simply the healthiest cuisine on the planet. No matter where you are in your dietary progress, you can benefit from knowing how to prepare fruits and vegetables correctly. You can eat better, and make your meals taste and look better.

There is a lot more you can do with raw fruits and vegetables than you could possibly imagine. Almost any cooked recipe could have a raw counterpart, and it would probably taste better! I have created raw pasta, crackers, pies, ice cream, and even lasagna!

The approach I took with this book is quite unique. Not only will I show you great recipes, but I will also show you the basic idea behind making these recipes, so soon you will be able to make your own recipes without the book.

Many authors sit down to write a recipe book thinking to themselves: "I'm going to show people how to make my best recipes. I will show them all of my little tricks and secrets, but they will never be able to make them taste as good as I can (laughter of the author fades)."

When was the last time you took a class with a chef, or borrowed a recipe from a friend who is really good with food preparation? Do you remember what happened when you came back home and tried the recipe yourself? It didn't taste as good, right? Why? Is it because you are not talented, or that cuisine is just not your thing? No, it is most likely that you did not understand the principles that make food creations great, and you just followed what was written on paper.

In this book, I will not only show you great recipes, but also how to make your own from scratch. It is not enough to just have the right ingredients and proportions, because there is more than that involved in making great food.

I hope you will join me for the ride, and experiment with the recipes contained in this book. At first, you might feel more comfortable following the recipes as they are written. If that is the case, then do so. Pick up a few recipes every day and enjoy making them. Then, try making the recipes without following quantities, just by looking at the ingredients. The next step is to experiment with new ingredients. No tomatoes? No problem, use some cucumbers instead. No cinnamon? Try allspice or cloves. Experiment with something new. The last step is not to use the book at all, but just pick up whatever you happen to have in your kitchen and create something delicious.

In the next part of the book we will explore the wonderful world of fruits and vegetables. All the ingredients used in this book will be discussed. Then I will show you what equipment is needed to make the recipes in this book.

At the end of the book, you will find a lot more information on the **Sunfood Diet**, relating to such important topics as organically grown food, and how to transition to the **Sunfood Diet**. The resource section will be of great help to further your progress with your healthy lifestyle, as you will be able to connect with all of the important organizations dedicated to the cause.

So have fun, enjoy your food, and live each day as an adventure!

An electromagnetic Kirlian photo of a kiwi cut in half
(photo by Christopher Wodtke, www.kirlian.com)

PART 2: THE INGREDIENTS

CHAPTER 3: SWEET FRUITS

Note: The seasons given in the descriptions of the fruits and vegetables apply to the Northern Hemisphere.

Apple — There are more than 150 varieties of apples in cultivation. Apples are one of the most healthy, simple and pure foods. "An apple a day keeps the doctor away" is a popular saying, meaning that apples contain certain compounds that help maintain health, clean the teeth, and satisfy the appetite.

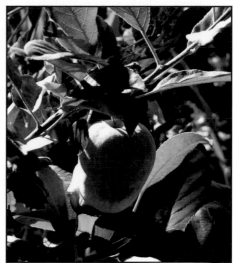

The apple can be one of your top ten most eaten foods. They can be easily brought along to work or on trips. They are so easy to eat, and do not make a mess like juicier fruits sometimes do. Another reason to eat plenty of apples is that organic apples are available in almost any health food store. Organic apples are even sometimes available in regular markets. Beware of non-organic apples, as they are heavily sprayed and waxed.

There are many varieties of apples in cultivation, so do not just limit yourself to the common "Red Delicious." The best varieties are often the tart ones, or sweet-tart, such as the Baldwin, Fuji, Cortland, Empire, and Gravenstein varieties. Select apples that are firm and vibrantly colored. You can often judge an apple by smell, but sometimes good apples do not have a distinct smell. Make sure they do not feel greasy, as this often means that they have been waxed. Bruises and imperfections do not matter, and may be a good sign! Organic apples do not look as "perfect" as the non-organic ones that often look more like a decoration than they do a real food.

Health benefits: Apples are one of the best fruits, mainly because they contain a moderate amount of sugar that does not rush into the blood stream too quickly. They have plenty of fiber, which acts as a broom in the intestines, insuring good bowel movements. Apples contain malic acid, which cleanses the liver, and helps to maintain healthy bacterial activity in the intestines. They also contain pectin, which helps to prevent the putrefaction of protein.

Season: August (early apples) through May. Apples store extremely well.

Apricot — Ripe apricots are hard to find in the stores. Unripe apricots can be starchy and give you indigestion. When you are able to find truly ripe apricots, preferably right from the tree, go for it! Ripe apricots are excellent in fruit salads, blended into smoothies, or simply eaten whole.

You might think that a nearly ripe apricot would ripen at room temperature, much like a pear or avocado, but that is not the case and they need to be purchased fully ripe. A fully ripe apricot is deep golden-orange in color with no trace of green, and slightly soft to the touch. A red tint is also a good sign.

Apricots originate from China, where they are widely cultivated. They are members of the drupe family, along with other stone fruits such as peaches, plums, cherries and almonds (which are a nut).

Health benefits: Apricots are a mild laxative, are rich in beta-carotene, and an excellent source of copper, cobalt, and iron. They are a mineral-rich food that is very useful in cases of blood-related diseases.

Season: Apricots are available from May through August (at best).

Banana — Bananas are one of the few fruits found in stores everywhere in the world. Although they are more likely to be grown in tropical countries, banana trees can be grown anywhere that does not experience freezing temperatures, although it will take much longer before they produce fruit. Bananas are also greenhouse-grown in countries like Iceland.

Bananas are a good food for those transitioning into a raw-vegan diet because bananas are high in sugar (with some starch), and are both filling and satisfying.

We have tried not to include too many bananas in the recipes of this book, because typical bananas are hybridized (do not have seeds), and contain a lot of starchy sugar. But due to the expansion of the organic food movement, many brands of exotic organic bananas are becoming a standard item on the shelves of health food stores.

Culinary speaking, there is nothing like the banana to enhance the flavor and add consistency to a smoothie. They are also good when eaten with other dried fruits, and in fruit salads.

Health benefits: Bananas are an excellent source of potassium, as many people know, and of other minerals and nutrients. They are rich in sugar, and are a good food for the very active person.

Season: Bananas are available all year.

Wild Bananas with Seeds

Blackberry — Blackberries belong to the same family as the raspberry. There are many varieties both in cultivation and growing wild. The wild varieties are especially delicious, and are found in abundance in temperate regions. You will recognize ripe blackberries with their deep black color, softness, and aromatic smell.

Health benefits: Blackberries are a good blood cleanser. They are rich in many minerals.

Season: May through August (may vary according to the location).

Carob — Carob is a pod-shaped fruit, brown in color, and used mainly as a chocolate substitute. It is sweet but not juicy, and can be eaten fresh as well as in a powdered form. Carob originates from the Mediterranean region of Europe. It is mentioned a few times in the Bible.

If you get the chance, try fresh carob. You will have to pick it from a tree, as it is not sold anywhere that I know of. It is a really satisfying food that fills you and takes care of any chocolate craving. The taste of carob is comparable to chocolate, but it does not contain caffeine, and has more minerals and less fat than chocolate. While chocolate is a stimulant, carob is calming.

Health benefits: Fresh carob pods are the perfect remedy for indigestion, diarrhea, and excessive flatulence. They are rich in calcium, and are perfect for building strong bones.

Season: Fresh carob is in season from September through December.

Cherimoya — If there is a fruit that is totally under-rated and under-cultivated in the world, it is the cherimoya. They are a member of the *Annona* family, in which we find the sugar apple, soursop, custard apple, and cherimoya, originating from South America. The cherimoya is usually round-shaped, or shaped like a heart. It is light green in color, and sometimes becomes darker as it ripens. Inside the fruit is a white, sweet flesh, which contains many shiny black inedible seeds. The flesh tastes like a mixture of banana, pineapple, and blueberry. Cherimoyas are grown in California, and can be found in some farmers market, health food stores, and exotic fruit stores. They are usually expensive, but are well worth the price.

Cherimoyas can be bought unripe and left to ripen at room temperature on a sunny windowsill—much like an avocado. To eat them, wait until they yield to gentle pressure, then break them apart in your hands. Eat the white flesh, discarding the peel and seeds. You can also use the flesh in smoothies and fruit salads.

Health benefits: Cherimoyas are high in calcium and many trace minerals.

Season: November through April (sometimes up to June).

Cherry — Is there a more beautiful fruit than a deep red cherry growing in pairs? Its aspect has inspired poets and artists throughout the ages. Cherries are a reminder of spring and all the splendors it brings. Cherries have a short season, so make sure you take full advantage of it, and eat as many as you can while they are available. Cherries originate from Eastern Europe and Asia, and are now grown throughout the world.

Select cherries that are bright, deep in color, and firm, with fresh stems. Avoid those that are too soft. Commercial cherries are heavily sprayed, and are often waxed, so make sure you buy organic cherries. Better yet, plant your own cherry trees.

Health benefits: Cherries are a good detoxifying fruit. I recommend that you try going a few days eating cherries only when they are in season. This will give your digestive system a rest, and make you feel great. This type of fruit fast is especially good to help conditions of gout, arthritis, rheumatism, and acidic stomach upset. Cherries have anti-putrid properties that help combat the effects of excess protein foods. They are rich in iron, as many red (blood) fruits are, and help to build healthy blood.

Season: May through July.

Date — Many people think of dates as a dried fruit. Although they can be dried artificially, they are naturally low in water, and do not need to be dried after being picked. However, many date distributors dry them further artificially, and then preserve them in glucose. The best dates are the juiciest ones, the ones available fresh at the stores in season. These soft ripe dates are exquisite compared to the dried dates most people are familiar with.

Good dates should still be moist, and not entirely dried. They should be plump with a shiny skin. Watch out for a fermented aroma, as this is a sign that the dates have spoiled. To prevent fermentation, dates may be frozen. Date trees grow in areas where temperatures are known to dip a little below the freezing point during the night, so keeping your dates refrigerated is normal for them.

The date is the fruit of a variety of palm tree that grows in desert climates. It is grown throughout the world in countries that enjoy a desert-like climate. In America dates are grown in California and Arizona, where many organic farmers are dedicated to growing the best dates in the world. Did you know that if someone were to plant a date palm for you the day you were born, by the time you would have reached your 18th year, the plant would produce enough food to feed you entirely for the rest of your life? Not that eating dates, and nothing else, would be best, but it is an interesting fact.

The date is a fruit that is very high in sugar, in a form that enters the blood stream quickly, and therefore dates do not agree with people suffering with diabetes, hypoglycemia, or candida. People needing to limit their consumption of sugar should limit their intake of dates.

Health benefits: Because of their high sugar content, dates are a good food for active people. They are also good for people who are transitioning away from sugar and chocolate, as they tend to satisfy us in a way these junk foods did in the past. Dates mixed with coconuts and almonds seem to work very well as a replacement for chocolate and candy. Many health food stores sell natural date "cakes," which are a good choice over any other artificial dessert. Powdered date sugar is available in many health food stores, and is an excellent replacement for, and has more nutrients than, cane sugar.

Season: Fall through Winter.

Fig — The fig is one of the most amazing fruits on the planet, and one of the fruits highest in calcium and other minerals. They originate from Mediterranean countries, and are grown in California, Greece, Turkey, and other countries that enjoy a warm climate.

Ripe, fresh figs can be found in many markets, health food stores, and exotic produce stores. Ripe figs are soft and slightly wrinkled. There are several varieties of figs, the most popular being the Black Mission (black-blue) and Calimyrna (yellow-white). Although you may sometimes find fresh figs at the store, nothing compares to the experience of eating a fig right off the tree. If you wait until they are at their most ripe and delicious state, as they just start to wrinkle and dry out on the tree, they will taste like grandmother's best jam.

Health benefits: Figs are one of the sweetest fruits, and therefore constitute an amazing source of energy for active people. They contain more mineral matter than most other fruits. They are especially abundant in calcium, which make them a very alkaline fruit. They are excellent as a natural laxative. Their high mucin content and tiny seeds help clean toxins and mucus out of the system. Some studies indicate that figs help to kill pernicious bacteria while promoting the growth of friendly bacteria in the intestines. Dried figs eaten in moderation, (organic and non-sulfured) are also good when fresh figs are not available.

Season: August through November.

Grape — The grape is actually a berry growing on vines. Grapes have been grown for thousands of years in Mediterranean countries, and are now grown throughout the world. The varieties that are grown for making wine are usually not the same as those grown for eating. The leaves are edible, and may be marinated in water, soy sauce, or lemon juice, and used to wrap guacamole, nut pâtés, or other raw concoctions.

Grapes are one of the most cleansing fruits, and one abundant in minerals and vitamins. Choose plump fruit still attached to the stem. Color is important, so look for brighter colored fruit. Buy the seeded varieties, and avoid the seedless varieties, which have been developed by humans.

Wine is the result of fermenting raw grape juice. If no preservatives are added, wine can be considered a living food. Research shows that a little wine reduces the levels of cholesterol in the blood, and offers other health benefits. However, new research shows that the benefits might come from certain compounds found in grapes, and that we could get the same benefits from just eating the grapes. Whatever beneficial effects wine may have are overruled by the effects of the alcohol, which is a poison to the system. If you drink wine, make sure that it is organic and free of added sulfites. All wine has naturally occurring sulfites, but some wine-makers add additional sulfites.

Health benefits: Grapes are a very cleansing fruit. High quality seeded grapes rank at the top of the list as a medicinal food. The grape cure used to be very popular in Europe, and consisted of eating only grapes for 1 to 4 weeks. Many people have benefited from this fast. Grape seeds are rich in antioxidants, and can be chewed along with the grapes. Antioxidants, as you may know, are the super-heroes that fight free radicals, the little beasties that wreak havoc on our cells, and play a role in cancer and other degenerative diseases.

Season: July through November.

Grapefruit — While most people are familiar with grapefruits, many have not enjoyed them in their pure state. The way many people eat grapefruits is halved with a spoonful of sugar sprinkled on top. The way raw-vegans eat grapefruit is the way most people eat an orange — by tearing off the rind, and eating the perfectly proportioned sections. The trick to grapefruits is to let them sit for a week or two before eating them — either on a sunny windowsill or in a safe place outdoors. They do not go bad quickly, and the extra ripening time allows for the rind to become firmer, and thus easier to tear off.

Health benefits: Grapefruits have powerful cleansing effects, and are especially good to get rid of inorganic calcium deposits in the body (as in arthritis) that result from the over-consumption of grain products and meat. It is a good fruit for those who have a hard time controlling their sugar level.

Season: Winter and early Spring, but they are available all year round.

Kiwi — Kiwis were not well known until the 1970's when they began to be imported from New Zealand. They originate from China, and are now widely grown in California. Named after the Kiwi bird of New Zealand, these fuzzy fruits are commonly used in fruit salads, but are also good eaten by themselves. While it is common to peel the skin off of kiwis, some people eat them whole, skin and all. Ripe kiwis yield to gentle pressure. Organic kiwis have a much better taste than chemically grown kiwis, which are sprayed heavily.

Kirlian photo of a kiwi (photo by Christopher Wodtke, www.kirlian.com)

Health benefits: Kiwis contain enzymes that help aid in digestion. They also are one of the richest sources of vitamin C.

Season: November through April.

Lemon —The lemon originated in China or India, and is now grown in warmer climates throughout the world. Used for their juice, lemons are an indispensable ingredient in **The Sunfood Cuisine**. Use them freshly squeezed on many dishes and salads, or in water. Select lemons that are semi-soft and feel "full" and heavy, with a bright yellow color. Do not be afraid to purchase lemons that are large or oddly shaped — these are likely to be of a less hybridized variety.

Health benefits: Lemons are important tools for detoxification, acting like solvent and dissolving mucus in the body. Drink one or two glasses of water with lemon squeezed in it every morning. This will help your body continue its cleansing actions that it was active doing during the night.

Season: Winter and Spring, but they are available all year round.

Lime — Because of their flavor, I prefer limes to lemons. When left to ripen long enough on the trees, limes become yellow. Although they are good green, their flavor is amazing when they are fully ripe (yellow). Limes that fall off the tree usually have a circular "burnt" tint at the bottom. This is a sign that they were allowed to fully ripen on the tree. Select limes that are closer to yellow in color. The use of limes is the same as lemons.

Health benefits: Same as lemons.

Season: Winter and early Spring, but available all year when imported from various locations.

Loquat — The loquat is a little spring fruit growing in California and other sunny climates. We are starting to see it more frequently in the fruit markets. It originates from Asia where it is more popular. The reason it has not been popular in markets elsewhere is because it is a tender fruit that needs special care during the picking and shipping stages.

Loquats at their prime ripe stage are really delicious. They have a flavor similar to grapes or pineapple. Ripe fruit are yellow-orange; the more bright in color the better. The skin of the fruit also tends to wrinkle while sitting on the tree, as the fruit starts to dry. Fruits in that stage are particularly sweet.

Health benefits: They are supposed to halt vomiting.

Season: May through June.

Mango — The mango is the world's most popular fruit. More children in the world know the word "mango" than "apple." They have been cultivated as far back as eight thousands years ago. The mango tree can reach an enormous size, and bear fruit for decades. Mangos are now starting to become popular in markets in America and Europe. As their popularity grows, their price is becoming more reasonable. Because of the increasing demand for this fruit, it is seen on store shelves throughout the world.

Mangos are a truly magical, sensual, paradisiacal fruit and they come in many sizes, shapes, and colors. The typical mango is about 1/2 to 1 pound, (225-450 grams). Ripe mangos yield to gentle pressure, and emit a very aromatic fragrance. I have found that the best way to select a good mango is by smelling it. Choosing by color is not always best, because there are some varieties that stay green even when they are ripe.

Health benefits: Because mangos are packed with both water and nutrients, they are useful for the kidneys, and as a general blood cleanser. They are a high energy fruit, and perfect for active people and children.

Season: April through September.

Melon — Melons belong to the same family as cucumbers and pumpkins, and grow on vines on the ground just like them. If you are one of those who lived all of your life in the city, it is time for you to know that melons do not grow on trees!

There are many types of melon. Among the most popular are the Watermelon, Cantaloupe, Honeydew, Galia, and Persian.

Selecting a perfect melon is not an easy task for a beginner. Some people use a "tapping" technique to determine if a melon is ripe. The idea is to tap the melon, and listen for the sound it makes. If it sounds hollow, or like you are hitting a jug of water, it is ripe. If it does not resonate more; it is not quite ripe. But personally, I think the best way to determine a good melon is by the smell and color. They should have a large white spot that indicates that the fruit has been sitting on the ground for a while. Also, the part where it was connected to the vine should give a little when you press on it.

There are also a lot of people who claim that melons should be eaten alone and not mixed with any other fruit. The idea comes from the food combining theory of Herbert Shelton that has been popularized in the book **Fit for Life**. Believers of this theory should read Dr. Shelton's work more carefully, to find that he actually said: "I have tried eating melons with fresh fruits, and there seems to be no reason why they may not be eaten together, if this is desired."

Health benefits: Melons are the perfect cleanser, and an excellent fruit for detoxification. They are rich in highly mineralized, distilled, organic water, and are ideal for hydrating the body during the hot summer months. They are excellent for people suffering from heart disease, because melons contain some compounds that help thin the blood. Another good thing about melons is that they require hardly any digestion. They pass quickly through the stomach and into the intestines for assimilation. They are no burden on the body, and are great for a mono-diet, during a detoxifying program, and as a food to start eating after a fast.

Season: Summer and early Fall.

Mulberry — The mulberry is the fruit of a shrub or tree that grows in many temperate climates. They have an incredible flavor when fully ripe, and are highly prized by birds, who often get them before humans do. They vary in size and color, as they can be white, black, purple, or red (sometimes two or three colors are seen on one berry). Selecting good mulberries is quite simple: they must be as bright, and as deep in color as possible, and soft.

Health benefits: They are high in iron, calcium, and many other minerals. They are a good food for helping stomach ulcers.

Season: June through August.

Nectarine — Nectarines are a popular fruit during the summer months in America and Europe. They are similar to the peach, but without the fuzzy skin, and with a flavor that some people prefer. There are many varieties, but the best ones are the white nectarines, which have a sweet white flesh. Good, ripe nectarines are slightly soft and give a sweet, fragrant aroma. They may also be purchased semi-hard, and left to ripen at room temperature on a windowsill. Commercial nectarines are rarely good as they are picked too early. For the best taste, look for tree-ripened nectarines. You are more likely to find them at a farmer's market.

Health benefits: Nectarines are rich in beta-carotene, and are an excellent digestive aid.

Season: June through August.

Orange — Oranges are native to China. They come in many varieties that are available throughout the year, mainly during the winter. The best oranges, sweet and delicious, are those that are kept longest on the tree to ripen. They might not look as "perfect" as other oranges, as they may be bruised and wrinkled, but they definitely have the fullest flavor.

The most common varieties of oranges include: **Navel**, the most popular that is available in the winter, and good to eat by simply tearing off the rind and eating the perfectly proportioned pieces one by one. **Valencia**, the variety that comes into season in the Fall, is used mainly for juicing, although they are also excellent to eat by hand. **Blood Oranges** are another really good variety of orange. You will recognize them by their skin spotted with tints of red and purple. The flesh of the blood orange is also tinted red or purple, and they have a tangy raspberry aftertaste. They are quite popular in Mediterranean countries. The *season* for blood oranges is *December through June.*

Health benefits: Oranges are high in calcium, and are a good body cleanser. The acids they contain help dissolve mucus in the body. Many people have used oranges on a mono-diet, either in juice or by itself, as a way to detoxify.

When going on such a program, remember that you should not eat too many oranges, as an excess of their acids may create problems. If you are doing the orange juice fast, dilute the juice with pure distilled water.

Season: Fall, Winter and Spring.

Papaya — The high life-force of papayas can be observed by the incredible speed that the seeds sprout and grow into a tree. It is common for papaya trees that are less than a year old to bear fruit. Papayas taste like a cantaloupe, but can have a consistency close to custard, and a very unique, musky flavor. They have been called the melons of the tropics.

Papayas originate from Central America, and are now grown all around the world in tropical climates. At the store, you will find basically two varieties: the smaller, yellowish Hawaiian papaya, and the bigger, orange-colored, Mexican papaya. Some people think that the small Hawaiian papaya has a better flavor than the Mexican one. This is not always true, as you can find really good Mexican papayas when they are truly ripe. Select a good papaya judging by its color. The deeper the color — yellow or orange — the better. Mexican papayas turning almost red-orange are really good. They are soft when ripe, and yield to gentle pressure. You can buy the fruit when it is still firm, and let it ripen at room temperature. Papayas can be found in many fruit markets around the world.

Health benefits: Papayas are a good body cleanser, help reduce gas, eliminate gastric indigestion, soothe irritation and inflammation, and help to cleanse and detoxify the system. They are especially rich in beta-carotene, calcium, and vitamin C. Green papayas are rich in enzymes that aid in breaking down protein. In many countries green papayas are cooked along with meat to tenderize it. You can add small chunks of green papayas (without the skin) to smoothies for an enzyme boost.

Season: All year round.

Passion Fruit — Passion fruits come in several varieties, including purple, sweet, giant, and banana. They grow on a vine, and are native to the Amazon. Passion fruits are about the size and shape of a large egg, and have a tough, cardboard-like shell. As they ripen, the shell becomes more and more wrinkled. As a general rule, the more wrinkled, the better and sweeter it is going to be.

Inside the shell, there is a juicy, slimy, yellow-orange pulp filled with edible seeds about the size of grape seeds. You can poke a hole into the passion fruit and suck the edible part out, seeds and all. Because the seeds are difficult to chew, most people simply swallow them whole. You can also cut it in half, and eat it with a spoon. Adding some orange juice makes it particularly delicious. The unique flavor is appealing, musky, guava-like, and sweetish-tart. It is strong, tangy, and really good when at its prime ripe stage.

Health benefits: Passion fruits are an excellent source of iron.

Season: Fall.

Peach — Peaches are native to China, and are now cultivated throughout the world. They are a delicious fruit when ripened on the tree, but unfortunately, they are not often sold in this perfect condition. In some places you may find tree-ripened peaches or, even better, get them directly from the farmer.

Select peaches that are firm and yield to gentle pressure. They should have a really pleasant aroma, and be vibrantly colored. Of course it all depends on the variety, since there are hundreds of them. Personally, I prefer white peaches to any other varieties that I have tried so far.

Health benefits: Peaches are a good diuretic. They are excellent for the complexion and the hair. A natural laxative, they aid in cleansing the system, especially when dealing with kidney and bladder troubles.

Season: June through August.

Pear — Pear or apple? My favorite is apples, but sometimes a perfect pear is hard to beat. Some of the many varieties of pear include: Anjou, a popular winter pear; Bartlett, a summer variety; Bosc, a long, dark yellow, or brownish variety that is super sweet when left to completely ripen (they do not need to be crunchy like everybody thinks); Comice, one of the sweetest and more flavorsome varieties. Chinese or Asian pear is a different type of fruit that has the flavor of a pear (and somewhat of the orange), and the crunchiness of an apple.

Pears will ripen off the tree. If your store does not sell ripe pears, simply purchase unripe ones and let them ripen at room temperature. They are at their peak when they have a creamy texture that dissolves in your mouth.

Health benefits: Pears are good cleansers and valuable for people with sluggish bowels. They are rich in alkaline minerals, and help overcome acidic conditions.

Season: August through April.

Persimmon — Persimmons originate from China, and are starting to be more popular in America. They look like orange tomatoes, and are ready to eat when they are as soft as an overripe tomato. Otherwise they are astringent, and will dry out your mouth faster than anything. In their ripe stage (super soft), they are very sweet, much like jam. The most common variety is called Hachiya.

I must reiterate that persimmons must be eaten super-soft! Softer than you might think. There is one variety, called the Fuyu that can be eaten when crunchy. This variety, however, can still benefit from longer ripening.

You can buy persimmons unripe, and let them ripen at room temperature. To hasten the process, you can place them in a paper bag in a dark, warm spot.

The wild persimmons that grow in some parts of the United States are smaller than the oriental varieties. They are not as juicy, but are sweeter. They have a richness in their sweetness that reminds me of dates.

Health benefits: Persimmons are one of the richest sources of beta-carotene, and tend to have mild laxative properties.

Season: December through February.

Pineapple — Pineapples originate from South America, and are now grown throughout the tropical areas of the world. You probably know how to recognize a pineapple, but do you know what a ripe pineapple looks like? The green pineapples you find in the store certainly do not deserve their name. A ripe pineapple is golden-yellow.

When you purchase a pineapple, look for those imported by aircraft ("jet-imported"), and that are yellow-gold in color. Smell them at the base — they should have a very sweet, aromatic fragrance.

You can eat pineapples plain, add them to salads, or juice them. Maybe you think that pineapples are too acidic. If so, try eating a ripe (yellow) pineapple, and you will realize you can eat much more before feeling that burning sensation in the mouth, which is the pineapple's way of telling you that you have eaten enough. If you eat too much pineapple, you can experience a sore top of your mouth, so be careful, and eat them in moderation.

Health benefits: Pineapples are rich in "bromelin," a protein-digesting enzyme. This is the powerful enzyme that causes the burning in your mouth if you eat too much pineapple. Pineapples are good for digestion, and as a diuretic. They are also very rich in vitamin C.

Season: Available all year round.

Plum and Prune — Plums are another summer fruit that can only be fully appreciated when they have been allowed to ripen on the tree. Most stores sell plums that have been picked prematurely. Plums come in all colors, including red, maroon, black, pink, green and yellow. All of the varieties differ in taste and shape. Select tree-ripened plums that are plump, fully colored and fragrant. The European plum is believed to be native to Asia.

Health benefits: Plums are a laxative and a stimulant. They are a high-energy fruit that is good for the nerves. Because they are rich in some acids (including oxalic acid), it is better to eat plums in moderation. Dried plums are called "prunes." Plums and prunes are a rich source of iron.

Season: June through September.

Pomegranate — Pomegranates are native to Persia. They are mentioned in classical mythology, the Bible, and the teachings of Mohammed. They are also featured in the archaeology of Solomon's temple, and in Tarot cards. They are often given as gifts to newly married couples because pomegranates are thought to be good for sexual toning and to promote fertility.

Pomegranates are grown in California, and in many parts of the world with sunny climates. They are a wonderful reddish-brown fruit that is often found dried in art and craft stores where they are sold for use in holiday ornamentation and seasonal decorations. Many people are so used to seeing pomegranates as a decoration that they do not recognize them as a food. While there are miniature pomegranates, the ones that are usually sold for eating are about the size of a large orange. A good quality pomegranate will have a thin, tough, and unbroken skin — a broken skin is indicative of a tree that did not receive enough water, but the fruit may still be good. The inside of a pomegranate contains hundreds of jewel-like, pea-sized, crimson, transparent seeds filled with juice, and that burst at the lightest bite. The juice has a tart flavor that is somewhere between the taste of a cranberry and strawberry. The seeds are good eaten by themselves, or tossed into salads. They also add a wonderful flavor to guacamole. The juice of the seeds may be used in all sorts of dishes, such as puddings, syrups, and marinated vegetables.

To open a pomegranate, cut the crown off, and soak the whole fruit under water for about 15 to 30 minutes. Break the pomegranate open under water and the seeds will fall to the bottom as the pulp floats to the top. To juice the seeds, simply mix them in a blender, then strain the juice to remove the seed casings. Whole pomegranates, or just their seeds, may be refrigerated or frozen. The juice lasts for five days under refrigeration, or six months when frozen, and can be used to make tasty ice cubes.

Health benefits: Pomegranates have been used to treat sore throats, skin inflammations, rheumatism, and dysentery. Scientists in Japan have found pomegranates to be beneficial for women who experience severe menopausal symptoms. Pomegranates have no fat, lots of fiber, and are a good source for a variety of nutrients, including vitamin C and potassium. They have many beneficial trace elements. They contain more antioxidants than grapes, and may be more effective than red wine in preventing heart-related diseases.

Season: July through November.

Prickly Pear — Also know as the Panini, or the Cactus fruit, this fruit owns its name for good reasons. It grows on a cactus, and is native to Central America. It is smaller than a pear, and wears small thorns on its peel. The ones you buy in the markets usually have had their thorns removed, so they can be handled safely. But be cautious nonetheless.

To eat a prickly pear safely, you have to peel them with a knife. You can peel it, or cut it in half, and eat it with a spoon. It tastes similar to a melon, but with many hard seeds inside. Not everyone agrees on what should be done with all these seeds. Some say we should spit them out, others say we can swallow them. I personally choose to swallow them. I guess you should avoid eating too many, so you do not get a blocked intestine.

Prickly Pears usually come in two colors: green or red. They are both good. To choose ripe fruits, look for those that are tender but not squishy. They are best when they have a deep, even color.

Health benefits: Prickly pears are rich in calcium, and are a beneficial food for people with sugar sensitivity problems, because of their low sugar content.

Season: Fall.

Raspberry — Raspberries are a popular berry that are cultivated, but also grow wild in many parts of the world. Most people think all raspberries are red, but there are also black, yellow, and white varieties that may be more delicious than the red variety.

Although you may find quality raspberries in the store, try to get the wild ones if they grow where you live. They are likely to be a lot sweeter and so much better nutritionally than the cultivated varieties. On average, the wild raspberries have more minerals and other nutrients than those grown on farms.

Health benefits: Raspberries are rich in calcium, iron, and other minerals. They are good system cleansers. They can help clear out accumulated mucus in your body, especially when you dedicate a few days to a raspberry cure— eating only berries and drinking water. This should prove to be an interesting experience, as you will save money that would have been spent on store-bought foods, while allowing your system to both rest from food, and work to dispose of accumulated toxins.

Season: July through August.

Strawberry — Strawberries are the most popular of all berries. They are also the most hybridized and rank high on the list of produce grown with pesticides and fertilizers. The wild strawberry is a lot smaller than the cultivated variety, but is often sweeter and, as with all fruits, has much better nutrition than the cultivated one. When purchasing strawberries, judge them by their color and smell. They should be deep red, and have a wonderful aroma. Avoid the ones with green or white tips, as well as the overly large, super hybridized varieties. And, of course, always purchase organically grown strawberries.

Health benefits: Strawberries are renowned as a skin-cleansing food. They are a rich source of vitamin C.

Season: Summer.

Tangerine — Tangerines are a delicious citrus fruit, usually much tastier than oranges. Tangerines peel easily, and have a wonderful flavor that is more rounded, but similar to the taste of oranges. Good tangerines have lots of seeds in them, which is always a sign of a good, healthy citrus fruit. If you like their flavor better, feel free to use tangerines for the recipes in this book where oranges are listed as an ingredient.

Health benefits: Same as oranges.

Season: Winter.

Watermelon — Although watermelons are no different than other melons, I thought they should be discussed separately as they are truly the queen of all melons. Watermelons are without a doubt the ultimate refreshment during the hot summer months.

They are native to the tropical regions of Africa.

During the past few years, many watermelons sold in stores are of a human-altered seedless variety. This hybridized version is nothing to be proud of. Seedless fruits tend to be unbalanced in minerals and high in sugar. Seedless fruits do not taste as good, and have no nutritional advantage over seeded fruits — especially with the watermelon, as its seeds are actually nutritious.

Health benefits: Watermelons are cooling and hydrating. Their high-quality water is useful in cleansing the digestive and blood systems. They are a powerful diuretic, which will help wash the bladder out in no time. Watermelon juice is often indicated in many detoxification programs. The rind can be juiced with the fruit to lower the sugar content of the juice.

Season: Summer.

Apple

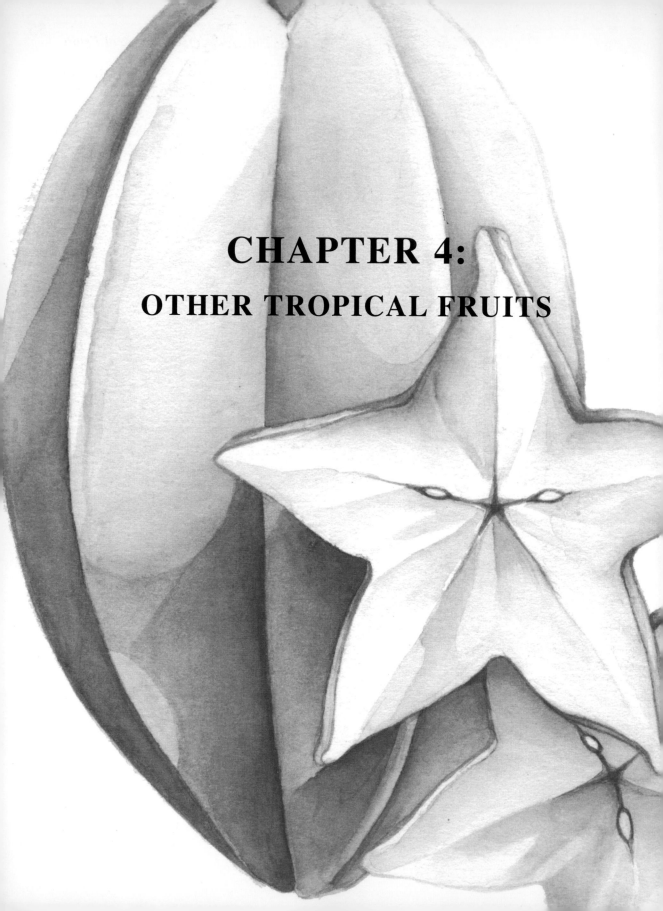

CHAPTER 4:

OTHER TROPICAL FRUITS

There are many tropical and exotic fruits worth trying. The following fruits are very popular in some countries, but are not well known in the Western world. I have been able to find all of them in Asian markets, and in specialty stores in the United States and Canada. To find these fruits, ask the people who work in the produce section, especially in stores where you have seen fruits that you are not familiar with. Ask which fruit they are, and what they taste like. Also ask about any other unusual fruits that you may see available. The people in the produce section are frequently excellent sources of information about how to eat the various fruits that they sell.

Carambola — This fruit originates from Sri Lanka and the Moluccas, and has been cultivated in Asia for a long time. It now grows in many tropical countries. The fruit is 3 to 6 inches long (7 to 15 centimeters), and its waxy skin turns yellow-orange when ripe. Inside there are only a few seeds and the fruit is eaten with its skin. It is very juicy, sweet, and slightly acidic. It is also called "starfruit" because when the fruit is cut into slices, the slices thus obtained look like stars, and these are wonderful for decorating fruit salads and desserts.

Dragon Fruit — The Spanish name for the Dragon Fruit is pitahaya, and it originates from Nicaragua. You can often find these fruits in Asian markets. Dragon Fruit is definitely one of the most beautiful fruits. Depending on the variety, it may be red or yellow, and as large as a big mango. The fruit must still be firm when ripe. If you wait until it is soft, it will no longer be good. To prepare, you simply cut it in half, and eat the inside flesh with a spoon. The edible part is white, juicy, and has a very delicate taste. There are many small seeds about the size of those found in a kiwi, which are also eaten. The center of the fruit is the sweetest part.

Eggfruit —The proper name for this fruit is "canistel," but it is more often called "eggfruit." Some also call it "yellow sapote," or "canistel sapote." It is native to southern Mexico and Central America. The fruit is usually oval, and the size of a small apple. When ripe, the skin turns yellow-orange, and the fruit becomes very soft. It can be eaten with the skin, but is most commonly eaten peeled. The edible part of the fruit is creamy, very sweet, and has a texture similar to that of a boiled egg, which is how it got its name. Because of its high sugar content, it is one of the most high-caloric fruits.

Feijoa — The feijoa tree is native to South America, and is now grown commercially in California and New Zealand. It is also called the "pineapple guava," because the inside of the fruit tastes like a juicy, pineapple-flavored guava. It can be shaped like an egg or more elongated, and is green in color like an olive. Ripe fruits are soft and their skin is not edible. If they are not ripe, you white flesh in a separate bowl. This is a lengthy process, but worth the time spent. Then, once you have separated all of the white flesh from the seeds, you put all of the flesh into a blender and liquefy it. This creates a delicious cream that can be eaten with a spoon. In Asia they add milk to this preparation.

Sugar Apple — This is the English name given to a fruit that is native to South America. It can also be called "sweetsop," as opposed to the fruit called "soursop." The sugar apple belongs to the same family as the cherimoya, but has a different appearance. It is round, ovoid, about the size of an apple, and its skin is composed of knobby segments, often with a reddish tint. The inside looks similar to the cherimoya, with a sweet white flesh in which bathe many black seeds, but it is sweeter than the cherimoya, and has a slightly different flavor that is similar to rose water. It is usually eaten on its own, or mixed in fruit salads. It is rich in vitamins and minerals, including calcium.

Papaya

Tropical Fruits of Asia

An electromagnetic Kirlian photo of a starfruit (carambola)
(photo by Christopher Wodtke, www.kirlian.com)

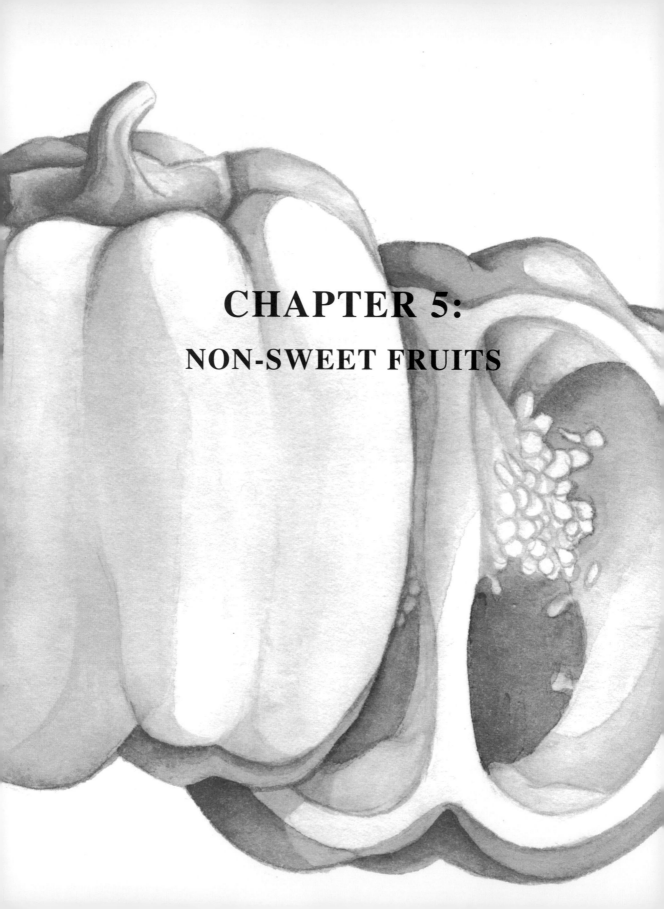

CHAPTER 5:
NON-SWEET FRUITS

WHAT IS A FRUIT?

Many of us think that fruits are the juicy, sweet gifts from the trees described in the previous chapter. But, as you will discover, the realm of fruit is much more vast than bananas and oranges. Did you know, for example, that pumpkins are a fruit? Did you know that avocados are also a fruit? Olives too? Yes, all of these and many more are fruits.

A fruit is a food that carries within itself the seeds for the reproduction of the plant. Fruits come from a flower, and by strict definition, fruit is the ripened ovary of a female flower. We like to think of fruit as a symbiotic relation between the plant and the fruit eaters. The tree (or the plant) wants to spread its seeds far and wide. So, instead of just producing seeds, it decides to wrap these seeds in some tasty and nutritious package. Then the fruit eaters come along, get attracted to the fruits, carry them around to eat them, and thus spread the seeds far and wide. If the seeds are swallowed, as in the case with the small edible seeds of tomatoes, figs, and other fruits, they are then carried even farther as they are transported in the intestines of the fruit-eating animal, and later released intact through the feces.

Most humans today do not have the same relation with fruit trees as their ancestors. Fruits are now predominantly grown on farms, picked by under-paid workers, sold at stores, bought by consumers and, after eaten, the seeds of the fruits are usually thrown into the garbage.

Some of the happiest people I have met are farmers who grow fruit trees using natural methods. I see them radiating an aura of peace and oneness with the Earth. I think this is because their life and sustenance revolves around what their trees produce — which is in direct relation to the blessings of Nature. I believe that it is good to go back to the days when we were more in tune with Nature and the goodness of the Earth. One way to do so is to grow our own gardens where we, like the fruit farmers, can learn how dependent we are on Nature. Planting, caring for, and enjoying the bounties of a garden, big or small, is something everyone should experience.

Cucumber — Although most people think of cucumbers as a vegetable (probably because they are used to eating them in salads), the cucumber is actually the fruit of a vine (like melons and squash). Cucumbers are especially refreshing in the summer, as their high water and low sugar content is perfect for hot weather. They are native to India and Egypt. There are basically three varieties of cucumbers: the long thin variety used in salads; the shorter, thicker, slicing cucumber also used in salads; and the small round one, used for pickling, but that is also excellent eaten raw.

Select a good cucumber by looking for firm, brightly-colored ones. Try out different varieties, and strive to find organically grown cucumbers. Cucumbers are one of the most heavily sprayed fruits and frequently waxed.

Health benefits: Cucumbers are a cooling alkaline fruit that also possess diuretic properties. Eating lots of cucumbers is known to facilitate excretion of wastes through the kidneys, and helps to dissolve uric acid accumulations, such as kidney and bladder stones. Their high potassium content makes them useful in dealing with conditions of high and low blood pressure.

Season: Summer and early Fall.

Eggplant — Like the tomato and pepper, the eggplant is a member of the night-shade family. It is called "aubergine" in France and the United Kingdom. The fruit is usually only eaten cooked. I have one use for it raw: you can marinate it in nama shoyu or tamari sauce, and create a raw "lasagna" (**See page 206**). Eggplants are believed to be native to South Central Asia, and possibly India. There exist many varieties, ranging from as small as an egg to as large as a football. The most common varieties in the United States are large and purple.

Health benefits: Eggplants are rich in bioflavanoids, which help renew arteries and prevent cardiovascular diseases. Eggplants are mostly water, and therefore, very cleansing.

Season: Summer and early Fall.

Okra — Okra is a fruit that originates from North Africa. It was introduced into the United States about one hundred years ago. It is very common in the south of the United States, as it is eaten cooked in some southern concoctions. When raw, it is slimy in consistency.

*Health benefit*s: Raw okra is rich in silicon, which is useful for the skin and bones.

Season: Summer and Fall.

Pepper — Peppers are native to South America. There are basically two types of peppers: bell peppers (sweet, mild peppers), and hot peppers (chile peppers). Both types of pepper come in different colors, but keep in mind that most green peppers are unripe. As the peppers ripen on the plant they become red, yellow or orange. But some peppers remain green even when ripe. The red (yellow or orange) peppers usually have a higher vitamin C content than green peppers.

Sweet bell peppers can be used in salads and other dishes, or eaten on their own, while hot chile peppers are used to spice a variety of dishes. Chile peppers come in many varieties, the most popular being jalapeño. Cayenne peppers are dried and dehydrated into a powder that is used as a spice. Whenever I use hot peppers in my recipes, I refer to jalapeño or cayenne powder. Feel free to use any type of pepper that you desire, to the degree of heat that you enjoy. Also, be careful when handling hot peppers. Remember to always wash your hands thoroughly afterwards.

Health benefits: Both sweet and hot peppers are rich in Vitamin C (up to six times as much as oranges). They also contain Vitamin B, which aids in food absorption, and normalizes the brain and nervous system. Hot peppers are antibacterial and stimulants. The active substance in peppers that gives them their bite is capsaicin, which stimulates the body to heal and cleanse. It helps clear parasites out of the intestines, normalizes blood pressure, improves the circulatory system, increases peristaltic movement, and helps the capillaries, arteries, and veins to gain more elasticity. Chile peppers are a wonderful medicine to take during the first months of your change in diet. You can juice them along with your vegetable juices, or add them to salads, salsas, and guacamole.

Season: Summer through Fall.

Tomato — The tomato is the most famous member of the nightshade family. It is native to South America, and is now eaten throughout the world. The fruit has been hybridized terribly, to the point where many tomatoes now found in stores are incredibly tasteless. Organic and homegrown tomatoes are always tastier than those sold in stores. There are many good varieties, most of which can only be found in home gardens. This is a good reason to consider growing your own tomatoes. They are quite easy to grow - you just need a sunny spot. When the season is over, and you have green tomatoes still hanging on the plant, you can pick them, wrap them individually in newspaper, and put them into a box. They will ripen, taking from a few weeks to a few months. When selecting tomatoes at the store, choose firm, plump ones, with a vibrant color. Avoid commercial tomatoes, as they are most likely to be genetically engineered, and chemically grown.

Health benefits: Tomatoes are a great mineralized, high water content food. But as with all members of the nightshade family, it is wise to not eat too many tomatoes, or at least to not eat them everyday, because of their oxalic acid content. Oxalic acid is an acid found in some fruits and vegetables which hinders the absorption of calcium. It is nothing to be feared — as it is only the abuse of the foods rich in this acid that creates a problem. However, people suffering from arthritic conditions should avoid foods from the nightshade family completely. This includes eggplant, potatoes, tomatoes, and peppers.

Season: Summer and early Fall.

An electromagnetic Kirlian photo of a tomato cut in half
(photo by Christopher Wodtke, www.kirlian.com)

Squash — Squash is an abundant fruit that grows on a vine, and comes in an incredible array of varieties—as many varieties as there are shapes. Squash is traditionally eaten steamed, baked, or cooked in stir-fries, mixed into casseroles, and used in soups. You will probably only want to eat the tastiest varieties in the living, raw state. Some popular varieties include banana squash, yellow squash, spaghetti squash, butternut squash, and zucchini. Zucchini may be the most popular member of the squash family, and is the most common type of squash in **The Sunfood Cuisine**. We use zucchini to make raw "pasta," as explained on **page 201**. Zucchinis are called "courgettes" in England, which is actually the French word for this fruit, meaning "little squash."

Health Benefits: Squash, as a highly alkaline, high water content food, are an excellent remedy for acidosis of the liver and the blood. Seeds of squash are helpful in expelling roundworms and tapeworms.

Season: Summer, Fall, Winter.

Cherry tomato

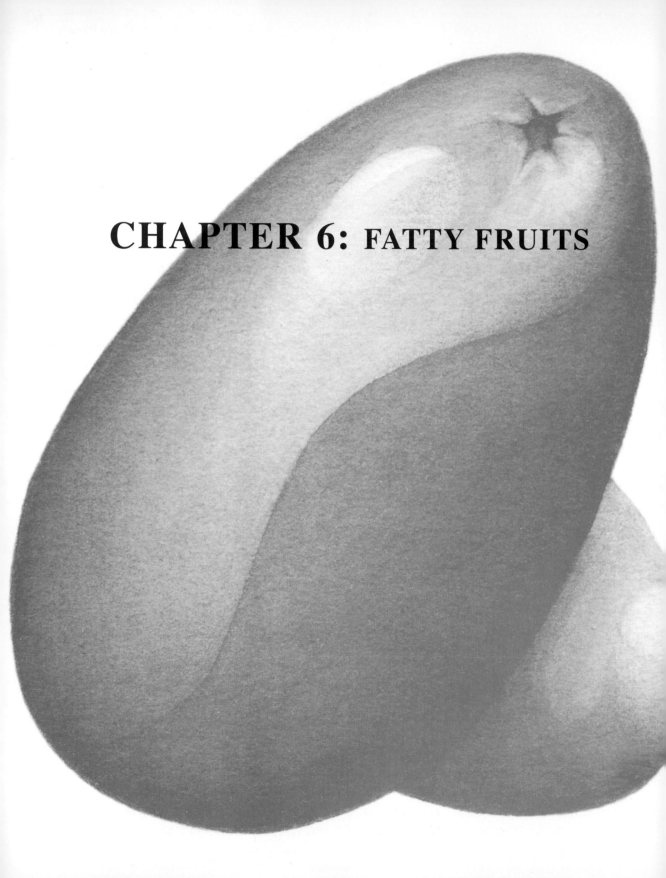

CHAPTER 6: FATTY FRUITS

Avocado — A staple in the raw food diet. Although many people consider them to be a member of the vegetable family, they are truly a fruit. The avocado trees originate from Guatemala, where they can still be found growing wild.

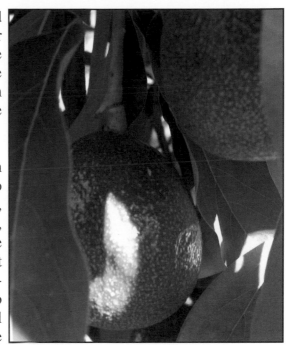

Many varieties of avocados are in cultivation. Do not limit yourself to Hass. If you can find other varieties, such as Fuerte, Reed, or Pinkerton, try them. Even if avocados can be purchased unripe and left to ripen at room temperature, you must understand that they are often picked too early, without letting the full oil content set in. Mature avocados are more bruised and imperfect-looking than immature ones. Sometimes immature avocados may be identified with a reddish tint on them, or a tendency to wrinkle without ripening. A good, mature avocado becomes quite fatty and can be enjoyed without seasonings. Ripe avocados yield to gentle pressure.

Health benefits: The avocado is a rich source of essential fatty acids. They are also rich in vitamin E.

> *Season: Depends on the variety. With different varieties overlapping each other, they can be found all year round.*

Durian — This is a fruit you probably have never heard of, and will probably be quite amazed when you see it for the first time. Imagine a roundish-shaped fruit, the size of a soccer ball, brown-gold in color, and covered with little spikes. Some people think it smells like rotten cheese, but tastes like vanilla custard. Although the smell of durian is quite strong and unusual, I do not consider it to be bad. In fact I like it.

Many people agree that eating a durian is one of the most intense food experiences you can have, although most cannot quite figure out how to eat it. First you should know where to get it.

Durian is grown in Thailand and Malaysia, where it is prized. In the Western world, it is imported and is commonly available in Asian markets in most cities.

There are basically three types of durian products available in stores. Fresh, whole-frozen, and package-frozen. Fresh durian is only available a few months a year (usually in the summer), and quite expensive. Expect to pay $20-$40 for one whole fruit. But it is worth it. Frozen durian is available all year round. It is picked ripe, and frozen whole. You will have to thaw it for 8-24 hours before eating. You may also find packaged durian, which is fresh, frozen durian flesh with no seeds, in a plastic container.

You might not like durian the first time you try it. This may be because you need to acquire a taste for it, or simply because you got a bad one. Selecting a good durian is not an easy task. So you may want to ask the people at the Asian market to pick a good one for you. If you want to try to pick one yourself, aim for those that are smaller and somewhat hevy for their size. The color should be more yellowish than greenish and the thorns large — the larger the thorns, the smaller the seeds. Try to squeeze two thorns together — it should be easy to do. There should also be a faint aroma of bittersweet butterscotch and almond with a bouquet of wild honey. Overripe durians split along lines of natural weakness which are faintly visible among the spines. To open a durian, insert a stout knife into such a line. Durians have about five segments, each containing several large seeds and the creamy custard-like flesh.

Health benefits: The durian is rich in essential fatty acids, high quality protein, and is reputed to be an aphrodisiac.

Season: All seasons, depending on the location.

Olive — Olives are a biblical fruit associated in the scriptures with symbols of goodness, happiness, purity and prosperity. In ancient Greece during the height of their culture Solon, the great lawgiver, enacted laws protecting all olive trees. He made it a capital offense to kill a tree or cut one down. The Romans were the first to perfect the stone-press with which they extracted the olive's oil. The Romans believed the olive to be an incredibly sexual fruit, an aphrodisiac— especially when eaten in large quantities.

Olives are usually picked green (unripe), and then pickled in a solution of water and salt (as a preservative). They can also be picked black (ripe), and left to dry in the sun. Most olives you find in stores have vinegar added, but it is possible to find some without it. Sun-dried olives have salt on them.

Olive trees are ubiquitous in the southwestern United States (California, Arizona and Nevada) as well as throughout the Mediterranean world, the Middle East, and India.

Health benefits: The olive is high in minerals, especially calcium. It is also rich in vitamin A and E. Olive oil can be used externally.

Season: Olives are available all year round, but are picked in the Fall, because this is when they are ripe.

*An electromagnetic Kirlian photo of a drop of olive oil
(photo by Christopher Wodtke, www.kirlian.com)*

CHAPTER 7: DRIED FRUITS

Fruits can be dried under the sun or in a dehydrator, and then stored for long periods of time in a cool, dry place. Although the dehydration process damages or destroys some nutrients, fruits and vegetables that have been dried at a low heat still retain some raw vitality. Thus dried fruits can be used during the long months of winter, when most fresh fruits are not available. Dried fruits constitute a source of concentrated energy, and should be eaten in moderation due to their high sugar content. Dried fruits may be used to create a variety of delicious living desserts that I include in Chapter 20.

When buying dried fruits, make sure they are organic and non-sulfured. Sulfur is an unhealthy chemical that is used in the preservation of commercial dried fruit for monetary reasons, as sulfured fruits are juicier and look better (according to the industry's standards). For example, the sulfured apricots you will find in the stores are those bright orange ones. Experiments conducted by Dr. H.W. Wiley, former chief chemist of the United States Department of Agriculture, demonstrated that the use of sulfurous acid in food is always harmful. It degenerates the kidneys, retards the formation of red corpuscles, and destroys the vitamins in the fruit. Real organic dried apricots are more brownish in color. The label should mention: non-sulfured. All dried fruits may be bought through the mail, from one of the companies listed in Appendix 4.

COMMONLY USED DRIED FRUITS:

Apricot — Some of the best sun-dried organic apricots come from Turkey. They are moist and sweet, and form a good little snack during the winter. Other excellent varieties are grown all over the world, including in California.

Raisin — The most popular dried fruit, raisins are now made using seedless grapes. Raisins used to have seeds inside of them, which added to their flavor and nutrition. But since humans have altered the plants, people have gotten used to eating raisins that lack seeds. About the only way you will get the best quality raisins is to dehydrate seeded grapes yourself.

Fig — Figs are a popular dried fruit. They are not too sweet, and have little seeds that give figs an interesting crunchy consistency when eaten. They grow all over the warmer climates, so there is always a fresh supply. They should be stored in a cool, dry place so that they do not ferment, or accumulate mold. They are rich in calcium, and are helpful for freeing constipation.

Prune — Some varieties of plums are cultivated to be dried as prunes. I believe they are the best of all dried fruits. Prunes are preferable to dates or other dried fruits because of their mineral content, and the fact that you will be less prone to overeat them, without facing some consequences. Although it is true that prunes act as a laxative for some people, I have found that when you have been on a raw food diet for long enough, you can eat a reasonable amount of them with no worries.

Other Dried Fruits Include: apples, blueberries, cherries, mangos, mulberries, olives, papayas, pineapples, and tomatoes.

CHAPTER 8: VEGETABLES

Artichoke — Artichokes are eaten cooked, and rarely raw. If they are very young, they can be eaten raw with delight. There is only a small edible part at the base of each leaf, as well as the base of the vegetable. You will have to cut it in half with a knife, in order to reach the good part. Artichokes are native to the Mediterranean.

Jerusalem Artichoke (also called sunchoke) is a different plant than the artichoke above. It is a plant native to North America that is eaten for its knobby root. It is similar to the potato, but much less starchy. They can be eaten sliced, or grated in salads and coleslaw, with a raw mayonnaise.

Health Benefits: Artichokes are diuretic, while sunchokes are good for diabetic people.

Season: Fall and Winter.

Asparagus — Asparagus is native to Europe, and now grows wild in North America and many other places. The spears can be eaten raw. Select them when they are young, fresh, sweet and tender. They should be bright green, straight, firm, and not too thick. The part that is good to eat is the tip, as the base is often too fibrous. You will find that they are a diuretic, and leave a distinct smell in the urine.

A Kirlian photo of asparagus (photo by www.kirlian.com)

Health benefits: Because of a substance called "asparagine," asparagus is an effective kidney diuretic. The asparagine breaks up oxalic and uric acid crystals that are in the kidneys and the muscles, and eliminates them through the urine.

Season: Spring.

Beans — Green (or yellow) snap beans are a popular addition to the garden that many people appreciate raw. I remember eating raw snap beans in my grandmother's garden during the summer as a kid, and never thinking that they would have been better cooked. They are best eaten straight from the garden, but if you buy them at the store, look for firm, long, slender, fresh, and vibrantly colored beans. Beans are believed to be native to the Mediterranean.

Health Benefits: Beans are rich in potassium, calcium, and minerals.

Season: Summer.

Health Benefits: Mustard greens are rich in calcium and other minerals. They help to alkalinize the body, as well as assist it in ridding itself of toxic substances.

Season: Fall, Winter, and Spring.

Onion — As Sanskrit and Hebrew literature indicate, onions have been culti- vated longer than most vegetables. Onions are often used for flavoring and can be added to many dishes. Green onions are the green leaves that sprout from the onion bulb, and are sold as a different vegetable. Shallots are used the same way as onions — in small quantities as a flavoring.

Health benefits: Onions are a wonderful food that possess antibiotic-like qualities, are a diuretic, blood pressure regulator, and antiseptic. Onions can be helpful in ridding the intestinal tract of parasites.

Season: All year.

Radish — Radishes are strong flavored bulbous roots. They are native to China, and have been eaten in Egypt since the beginning of their civilization. There are a few varieties available, the most common being the small red radish. Bigger, black radishes are also cultivated and are a variety that keeps well during the winter. Radishes are commonly used in salads, but can also be eaten on their own.

Health Benefits: Radishes are rich in sulfur, which is an important element for skin beauty.

Season: Spring, Summer, and Winter (for Winter varieties).

Shallots — See Onion.

Spinach — Spinach originally comes from northern Asia, and is now one of the most cultivated green vegetables. There are many varieties which are all excellent. Many people do not like spinach because of the way it is traditionally prepared: cooked. Raw spinach is much more pleasing to the palate. You can juice it along with other vegetables for a healthy drink. It is also good chopped and added to many different dishes, and blended into raw soups.

Health benefits: Raw spinach is an excellent food for detoxifying the digestive tract and restoring pH balance. It is rich in minerals, especially iron (as Popeye knew — although the cooked, canned spinach Popeye was eating would not be recommended). Spinach also contains a notable quantity of oxalic acid, and therefore it would be a good idea not to eat too much of it, or eat it too often, since oxalic acid is reputed to hinder the absorption of calcium. However, many people eat spinach every day, and do not seem to suffer any negative effects from this.

Season: Summer and Fall.

Sprouts — When you soak any seed in water, it sprouts, releasing all of its stored nutrients, enzymes, and life-giving potential. When this was discovered, the practice of sprouting the seeds of alfalfa, buckwheat, sunflower and other seeds in order to eat the young plant they produced became popular. Ann Wigmore was one of the first people to promote the health benefits of sprouts. Nowadays, you can find sprouts in most every food market, and as part of the food offerings in many restaurants.

Sprouts are useful for many reasons. Sprouts are vegetables that with a little time and investment are easy to grow. Sprouts are ready to be harvested within a week. With the knowledge of sprouting, good nutrition is now possible in the most extreme situations such as cold winters, food supply exhaustion, long trips in the woods or the ocean, etc. You can eat sprouts on their own, or mix them with salads.

Health benefits: During sprouting, the vitamin and enzyme content of seeds increases dramatically, while starch is being converted into simple sugars, and all the other nutrients become more assimilable. The fresher the sprouts are, the more nutritious they will be. So it is better to grow your own sprouts, which is quite easy to do. There are many books on the subject that can guide you in the process of sprouting a variety of seeds.

The best sprouts are those which turn into little green plants, such as sunflower greens and buckwheat greens. Some sprouts, such as bean and grain sprouts, will still contain high amounts of raw starch, which is not totally transformed into simple sugar. Because raw starch is difficult to digest, it is better to eat these starchy sprouts sparingly. The best varieties include clover, buckwheat greens, sunflower greens, fenugreek, mustard, and radish. The starchy sprouts include: wheat berries, mung beans, and chickpeas.

Season: All year. Sprouts may be grown at any time of the year in any climate, as long as a warm place with some light is provided.

Sweet Potato & Yam — These tubers, although they are not related, have similar characteristics. The typical white potato is not used in **The Sunfood Cuisine**, due to the fact that it is highly hybridized and has a high starch content. But sweet potatoes and yams are closer to their wild ancestors, and are a staple item in many countries of the world. They may be eaten raw, grated in salads, or sliced as a dipping ingredient with guacamole or nut pâtés. Although you might think that raw sweet potatoes are not edible, you should try them at least once. Many Sunfoodists occasionally enjoy the taste of raw sweet potatoes and yams. The sweet potato is native to the southern United States, while the yam is native to West Africa and Asia.

Health benefits: Sweet potatoes and yams are highly nutritious, and very alkaline when eaten raw. They contain a high amount of beta-carotene, and other important nutrients.

Season: Fall and Winter.

CHAPTER 9: NUTS & SEEDS

Nuts and Seeds are a concentrated source of energy. While their use in the typical diet is often limited to snacks in a roasted and salted form, you will realize that nuts have a much more important role in **The Sunfood Cuisine**. Nuts and seeds are rich in minerals, trace minerals, and essential fatty acids. Most people are deficient in essential fatty acids, because the majority of the fat they eat is cooked. Heated fat, such as fried oil, is carcinogenic and simply not good for the body.

Ideally, nuts and seeds should be bought raw and organically grown. Nuts in the shell and whole seeds are more superior than shelled nuts and refined seeds. In recipes we prefer to use shelled nuts to save time. To make them easier to digest, nuts and seeds can be soaked in water for a few hours.

Nuts and seeds may be used in various ways. They can be eaten on their own (ideally with green vegetables) as a snack. They can be added to salads, turned into milks and pâtés, added to smoothies, and used in sauces and dips. Since nuts are acid-forming, they should always be eaten with green vegetables, which are extremely alkaline. For more information on acid/alkaline balance read **The Sunfood Diet Success System** by David Wolfe.

ABOUT THE SOAKING OF NUTS AND SEEDS

Many recipes in this book call for soaked nuts and seeds. We soak the nuts because it makes them easier to digest. Also, it is sometimes necessary to achieve the desired consistency in the recipes. I recommend that you soak your nuts and seeds the night before using them. Place a little more than half of the quantity you intend to use the next day into a bowl, and cover with purified water. They will almost double in volume. Do that before you go to sleep. The next morning, strain the water, rinse the nuts or seeds, and place in the refrigerator until you are ready to use them. You may also soak them in the morning for use in the evening. Plan on soaking them for 6-12 hours. If you do not have that amount of time, try to soak them for at least a few hours anyway.

NUTS

Almond — Most almonds available in North America are grown in California. Almonds are one of the sweetest of all nuts, and a popular ingredient in **The Sunfood Cuisine**. Almonds should be bought organic because non-organic almonds are likely to contain heavy doses of toxic chemicals. Almonds can be used to make delicious milks, nut butters, pâtés, sauces, and raw candies. The almond tree is native to North Africa, West Asia, and the Mediterranean.

Health benefits: Almonds are rich in calcium, as well as many other minerals which are useful for building up a body which is underweight. For best assimilation, almonds should be soaked and masticated thoroughly.

Season: Fall and Winter.

Brazil Nut — Brazil nuts grow wild in the jungles of South America. Even today, the Brazil nuts you purchase are likely to come from wild trees, which are huge evergreens whose trunks may grow up to six feet in diameter, and reach the immense height of 150 feet! These nuts have a pleasing rich flavor, and are one of the richest nuts in fat. It is preferable to buy them in the shell, as shelled Brazil nuts have been boiled to release them from their shell.

Health benefits: With their high fat content, Brazil nuts are useful for those doing hard physical work, or for individuals needing to gain some weight. They are acid-forming, and should always be eaten with green vegetables.

Season: Fall and Winter.

Cashew — Cashews are a seed that grow at the base of the fruit called the "cashew apple." The fruit contains a sweet liquid, and is used as a drink in the tropical countries where the cashew tree grows, mainly in Central America. The nut has to be slightly heated in order to get rid of some acids. I have heard that it is also possible to sun-dry the nut to achieve the same result. There is a lot of controversy concerning the cashew nut. Many believe that it is not a living food, since it has to be heated before consumption. If they sprout, then they can be considered alive (raw), otherwise they are dead (cooked). **Nature's First Law** is the exclusive distributor of raw wild cashews in the United States. Cashews can be turned into delicious nut milks **(page 155),** blended into smoothies, dressings, scattered into salads, made into nut butters or pâtés, or eaten on their own.

Health benefits: Cashews are rich in calories and therefore useful for the very active person, or the individual who needs to gain weight.

Season: All year.

Coconut — The coconut is the queen of all nuts. I say this because coconuts provide both solid and liquid food. It is a staple in the diets of the tropical countries where it grows. To get the nuts, someone has to climb to the top of the palm trees on which the coconuts grow. This is how coconuts have always been harvested, including those in your local supermarket. They are believed to be native from Polynesia, Malaysia, and southern Asia.

As coconuts ripen, the meat inside of them becomes firm. The brown coconuts sold in supermarkets are the "mature" coconuts, with a hard meat and sweet milk. When picked before that stage, the meat inside of the coconut is soft, and can be eaten with a spoon. These are then called "young coconuts," or "spoon-meat coconuts" and are white-husked. They are our favorite, and can be obtained at many Asian Markets. Many health food stores are beginning to carry young coconuts and, even if they do not, they may be willing to order some for you at the cost of about $1 to $1.50 each. Young coconut meat can be eaten plain, or blended into smoothies, soups, or dressings.

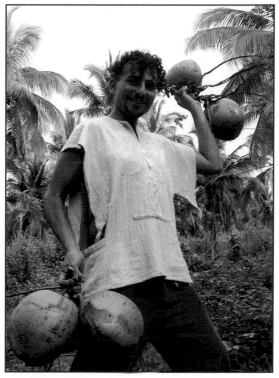

Homemade, freshly shredded coconut may be obtained by processing the meat of mature coconuts in a food processor or Champion Juicer. It can be used in the preparation of living desserts. Blending the hard coconut meat with its water, and filtering out bits of coconuts by pouring through a strainer makes coconut milk. It can be used as any other nut milk. Coconut water is the liquid inside of the coconut. It can be consumed as it is, or blended into soups or smoothies. Coconut cream is made by juicing the hard coconut meat with a Champion, Green Power, or Green Life juicer (or any other mastication or twin-gear juicer). It can be used in place of milk cream. Coconut butter is simply coconut oil. Since coconut oil is solid at room temperature, it has the appearance of butter. Coconut butter may be used in place of regular butter — as a transition food — and also used in place of other types of oils. It is high in saturated fat, which may be of concern to people with cholesterol problems. But it should be noted that there is no proof that saturated fat coming from a natural source, such as coconuts, cause any of the same health challenges as saturated fat coming from animal sources. Many nations eat plenty of coconut everyday, and do not suffer from the cholesterol problems seen in countries where saturated fat from animals is consumed. **Nature's First Law** distributes raw coconut butter, and it is by far the best coconut butter in the world!

In my opinion, one of the reasons why coconuts are the best nuts is that they are fresh. Many nuts available in stores have been dried, heated, or salted. With coconuts, you know that they are still alive and unprocessed.

Health Benefits: Coconut water is rich in calcium and trace minerals, and can be used to remineralize the body and provide sustenance with its sweet water. Coconut meat is rich in saturated fatty acids, and is a perfect body building food.

   Season: All year.

Hazelnut or Filbert — Different varieties of these nuts are native to North America, Asia, and Europe. They still grow wild across the northern part of the United States, and are grown commercially in the states of Oregon and Washington.

Health benefits: When eaten in combination with green vegetables, they form a wonderful body building food. They are also rich in calcium and trace minerals.

   Season: Fall and Winter.

Macadamia Nut — Macadamias are often the favorite nut of raw vegans due to their high fat content, brittle crunchiness, and incredible flavor. They originate from Australia, where they still grow wild. It has only been 150 years since farmers began cultivating these delicious nuts. They are usually more expensive than other nuts, and considered a delicacy by many people. But, because many farmers in California and Hawaii are now growing them, macadamia nuts have become less expensive, and more popular. The nuts are contained within a very hard shell, which resists most nutcrackers. There is one nutcracker that will do the trick, called the Krakanut. If you buy nuts in the shell it is a necessary investment! You can also buy them shelled, but as with all nuts, it is better to buy them in the shell, as they will be fresher.

Health benefits: Macadamia nuts are rich in all of the essential fatty acids, offer a better balance of these acids than most nuts, and contain a larger amount of the Omega-3 fatty acid, which is the one that we usually need more of. They also contain plenty of trace minerals, and form a great bodybuilding meal when they are eaten in combination with green vegetables.

   Season: Fall and Winter.

The Kirlian Field of a Macadamia Nut
(photo by Christopher Wodtke, www.kirlian.com)

Pecan — Pecans are native to North America, and still grow wild in some areas of the country. The trees are very long-lived, and some of them are thought to be over a thousand years old. Pecans have a fine flavor and high mineral content, which makes them appropriate in the creation of living desserts. Pecans are also delicious when added to salads, or simply eaten alone.

Health benefits: Pecans are one of the richest plant sources of vitamin B6, which plays an important role in the nervous system. Their mineral and fatty acid profile also makes them good for those needing to rejuvenate their heart.

Season: Fall.

Pine Nut — Pine nuts are the seeds from the cones of certain species of pine trees. They have the most delicate, buttery taste of all the nuts, and are used in many gourmet raw vegan meals. For added taste and nutrition, you can sprinkle them onto your salads, dips, and sauces.

Health benefits: Pine nuts are rich in quality proteins, and many trace minerals.

Season: Fall.

Pistachio — Pistachios are delicious nuts, which are appreciated in Middle Eastern countries. In America, salted pistachios are sold at sporting events. This nut has a unique and delicate flavor. We like to add them to salads.

Most pistachios found in markets, and even health food stores, are roasted, dyed, salted, or processed through other means. There are a few places that sell raw, natural pistachios —and they are listed at the end of this book.

Health benefits: Pistachios contain little fiber, and are therefore easy to digest and assimilate. Raw pistachios are useful in purifying the blood, and in helping to maintain a healthy liver and kidneys.

Season: Fall and Winter.

Walnut — Walnuts are one of the most popular nuts in North America. Many varieties of walnuts, including the black walnut, are indigenous to North America. Some varieties of walnuts include: Chinese walnut, Japanese walnut, white walnut (also called butternut) and English walnut.

Due to their high oil content, walnuts tend to go rancid quickly, and should be bought in the shell whenever possible. They should be stored in a cool, dry place. Walnuts may be added to salads, or used in nut pâtés, turned into milks, and used in raw desserts. I like to use walnuts as a base for raw pie crusts.

Health benefits: Walnuts are a good food for improving the metabolism, and for strengthening the kidneys and lungs. Black walnuts are an old proven remedy for ridding the intestines of parasites.

Season: Fall and Winter.

SEEDS

Flax—Flax is a plant grown for its fiber, which is used to make cloth (linen). The seeds of the plant are also cultivated, as they are highly nutritious. The tiny, shiny, dark brown or golden seeds may be ground and added to smoothies and dressings. They have to be ground beforehand, in order to be assimilable by the body. The seeds can be used to make flax crackers **(see page 209)**. We use their oil in salad dressings, soups, and other dishes to enhance flavor, texture, and to add essential fatty acids.

Health benefits: Flax seeds (and flax seed oil) are rich in Omega-3, an essential fatty acid (EFA). This EFA helps people with heart problems, and is also an important nutrient for the brain. Flax seeds also contain plant hormones, and are high in potassium, magnesium, calcium, iron, lecithin, and vitamin E.

Season: All year.

Pumpkin — Pumpkin seeds are very tasty and nutritious, and can be used in salads, nut pâtés, and soups. Also, they may be eaten as a snack on their own, or ground and added to salads. It is better to grind pumpkin seeds before adding them to salads, in order to get the maximum nutrition available.

Health benefits: Pumpkin seeds are rich in zinc and magnesium, which make them a most nourishing food for the sexually active male, as these minerals are used in the production of semen.

Season: Late Summer and Fall.

Sesame — Sesame is another popular seed. It is commonly consumed in the form of tahini, which is nothing more than butter made out of hulled sesame seeds. Unhulled seeds have a stronger taste than hulled seeds and are alkalizing. Hulled seeds are used mainly in the preparation of tahini. Tahini made out of unhulled sesame seeds is usually called "sesame butter." Sesame seeds come from a tall herb, and are grown in Africa and Asia. Tahini is a common food in Middle Eastern countries, while sesame oil is widely used in Chinese cooking. Whole, raw sesame seeds are great to use in raw candy, which can be made by mixing sesame seeds with blended dates, then rolling small balls of this into shredded coconuts and chopped nuts.

Health Benefits: Unhulled sesame seeds are rich in calcium, and may be ground and mixed with smoothies, or added to salads in order to add minerals to the diet. Sesame seeds are high in Vitamin E, which strengthens the heart and nerves.

Season: September through April.

Sunflower — Sunflower seeds grow on a majestic plant that is native to the Americas and that has been made famous by Vincent Van Gogh, who was fascinated by the beauty of the sunflowers in the fields of the French countryside. They may be used in nut pâtés, turned into delicious milks, or enjoyed as a snack on their own. The unhulled seeds may be sprouted and enjoyed as a nutritious green vegetable, when the plant has grown a couple inches tall with little green leaves. At that stage they are full of vitality and sun energy.

Health Benefits: The sunflower seed is a rich source of vitamin D, B complex, E, and K. They are also a rich source of high-quality protein.

Season: Fall and Winter.

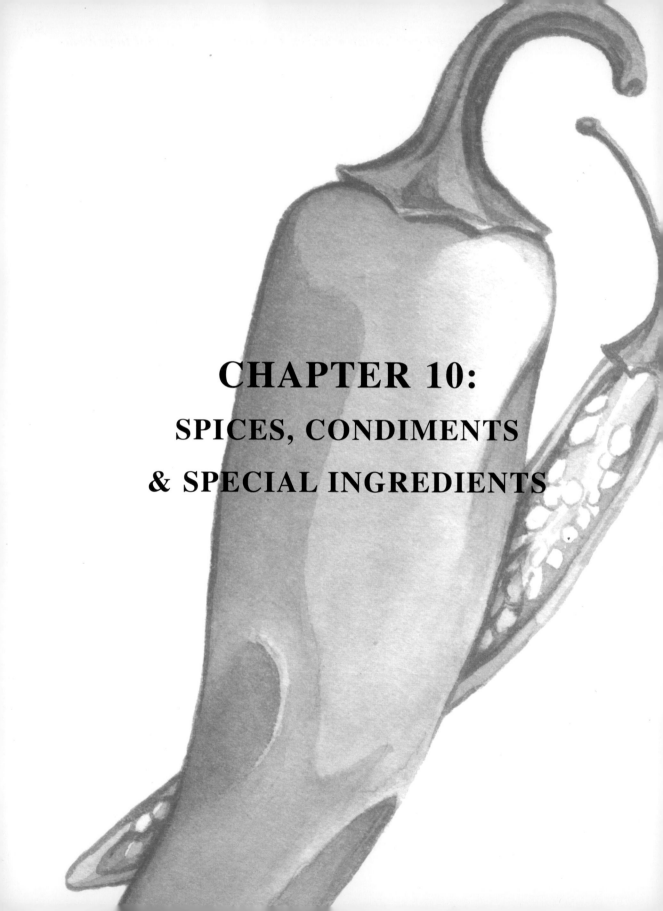

CHAPTER 10:
SPICES, CONDIMENTS
& SPECIAL INGREDIENTS

In this section we will discuss the spices, condiments and special ingredients that are used in **The Sunfood Cuisine**. Some of these ingredients may already be familiar to you, and others may not. You do not need all these ingredients to make great food, but I use some of them quite often — as you will discover by making the recipes in this book. Many of these ingredients may be bought at your local health food store.

Condiments can really make **The Sunfood Cuisine** sparkle. You may choose not to use them, if you prefer the taste of unseasoned food. Some purists may object to some of these items, saying that they are not "living" or raw. My response to this is, correct — some of these condiments are other than living. But they are used only for flavor, and in such small quantities that I cannot see how they could reduce the vitality otherwise attained through following a raw food diet.

HERBS AND SPICES

Remember that most spices and dried herbs are irradiated, so look for non-irradiated spices and always seek out those that have been grown organically. Many of these herbs can be obtained fresh at the market or from your garden. If you have access to fresh herbs, I recommend using them over dried herbs. If you substitute fresh herbs for dried herbs in one of the recipes, use 3-4 times as much of the fresh as the stated quantity of dried herbs listed in the recipe. However, I sometimes deliberately use dried herbs even though the fresh ones are obtainable. For example, the taste of powdered garlic is different than the taste of fresh garlic. Sometimes I like to use powdered garlic to achieve a particular taste in a recipe.

Basil — Also called sweet basil, it is native to India and Iran. There exist a few varieties including small-leaf common basil, larger leaf Italian basil, purple basil, lemon basil, and the large lettuce-leaf basil. It most often associated with Italian cuisine. It is excellent with tomatoes and in salads.

Cardamom — A spice consisting of the whole or ground dried fruit, or seeds, of a plant member from the ginger family, native to the moist forests of southern India. It a popular seasoning in Oriental dishes, and commonly used in the preparation of Chai, an Indian spiced tea.

Cayenne — Dried hot powder made out of the cayenne pepper, and used to spice a variety of dishes. Cayenne pepper is native to the warmer regions of Asia and America, and is now cultivated in all parts of the world. It is very spicy and should be used carefully.

Chili powder — A blend of spices, often containing cayenne pepper, oregano, paprika, cumin, and garlic.

Chives — A plant related to the onion, chives are native to Asia and Europe, and are grown for their tubular leaves which grow in clumps. They may be used to flavor soups and salads.

Cinnamon — A powder made out of the inner bark of a tree, excellent for flavoring anything sweet. It is one of the oldest known spices and is native to Sri Lanka. The spice is light brown in color and has a delicate fragrant aroma and warm sweet flavor. Cinnamon was once more valuable than gold. In the United States it is especially popular in baked goods. It can be purchased whole or in a powder form.

Cilantro — Native to the Mediterranean and Middle East regions, cilantro is cultivated in Europe, Morocco, and the United States for its seeds, which are turned into a powder called coriander. The fresh leaves are used in Latin American, Indian, and Chinese dishes. It can be added to all sorts of dishes. If fresh cilantro is not available, it can be replaced by fresh parsley.

Clove — The word "clove" comes from the French "clou," meaning "nail." The clove tree is believed to have originated in China. The spice comes from the buds of a tree, which are sun-dried and turned into a powder, or sold whole. Cloves are highly aromatic, and used to spice pies and nut milks.

Cumin — Cumin is native to the Mediterranean region, and also cultivated in India, China, and Mexico for its seeds, which are turned into a powder and used to flavor a variety of dishes. Cumin is an excellent spice to use in guacamole.

Curry — A combination of spices. The basic ingredients in curry powder are turmeric (which gives the yellow color), cumin, coriander, and red (or cayenne) pepper. It is popular in Indian cuisine.

Dill — A member of the parsley family, dill is native to Mediterranean countries and southeastern Europe, and now widely cultivated in Europe, India, and North America. It can be used for its leaves or seeds, which are very aromatic. It is very popular in Persian cuisine.

Fennel — Fennel is a plant that has a licorice flavor, and can be used as a flavoring. It originates from southern Europe, and now grows wild in various locations, including the United States. It is sold in a few stores as a vegetable, which can be used for its aromatic bulb, stalks, and leaves. Good in salads.

Garlic — Garlic is a bulb native to the Mediterranean regions of Africa and Europe. The bulb separates into segments that are called cloves. Garlic is considered one of the most important spices in healthy cuisine and we use it to flavor many dishes in **The Sunfood Cuisine**. Garlic keeps a long time when it is stored in a cool dry place. One thing you can do with the cloves is plant them in a pot, and use the flavorsome garlic greens in salads, soups, and as garnishes. Garlic is one of the best antibacterial and antiseptic plants. Eat raw garlic to rid the intestines of parasites. It can be used to boost the immune system, purify the bloodstream, and also regulate the action of the liver and kidneys.

Garlic powder — Powder made out of dried garlic cloves. Garlic powder has a slightly different and mellower flavor than fresh garlic.

Ginger — The ginger plant is believed to be native to southeastern Asia. It is grown for its aromatic underground stem, part of the plant which is called a "rhizome." People call it "ginger root," although it is not an accurate designation. It is used as a spice, flavoring, food, and medicine. Its use in India and China has been known from ancient times. Ginger can be used fresh or in a powder form. It is wonderful when used to enhance the flavor of many raw dishes, dressings, and juices.

Italian herb mix — A mix of dried herbs, usually consisting of oregano, marjoram, thyme, rosemary, basil, and sage. Usually sold under the name "Italian Seasoning."

Marjoram — A member of the mint family, used for its leaves and flowering tops, either fresh or dried, to flavor many foods. Marjoram is native to the Mediterranean. It tastes similar to oregano.

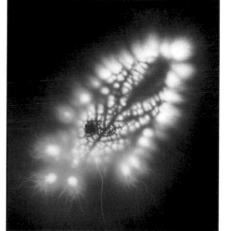

Mint — The mint plant, which is used for its aromatic leaves, is native to the Near East, and now grows all over the world. Mint leaves are refreshing, and can be used fresh or dried. I like to add mint to fruit salads and other desserts.

Kirlian Field of Mint

Mustard — Mustard plants and seeds are mentioned frequently in Greek and Roman writings and in the Bible. As a condiment, mustard is sold in three forms: as seeds, as dry powder, and as a paste that is blended with other spices, salt, and vinegar. I have been able to find a mustard condiment in some health food stores, made with mustard seeds, apple cider vinegar, and sea salt. It is made by a company called "Eden" and is much healthier than regular mustard.

Garlic-Chili flavored flax seed oil — A very tasty oil, flavored with garlic and chilis. It is made by an American company called Omega. But it can also be made at home by soaking a few garlic cloves and chili peppers in 2 cups of flax seed or olive oil.

Green olives — Green olives are often picked before maturity and pickled in a special solution that includes vinegar. Some olives are cured in water only. To get these olives, as well as other high quality sun-ripened olive varieties, contact **Nature's First Law.** You will find them listed in the Appendix.

Hemp seed oil — One of the most nutritious of all oils because it contains the perfect balance of essential fatty acids. Hemp seed oil has a pleasant, nutty flavor. It can be used with, or in place of, olive oil. It is now increasing in popularity, and is available cold-pressed in many health food stores.

Honey — Different types of honey are available, usually named after the flowers that fed the bees or after a town or region where the honey was gathered. There is wildflower honey, orange blossom, buckwheat, etc. Many varieties of honey sold on the market have been heated, which destroys the natural abundance of enzymes. The label "raw" does not mean anything as far as honey is concerned. It should mention "unheated." For those who object to honey for different reasons, you can replace honey in recipes with maple syrup or dates. For maple syrup, use twice the quantity. For dates, use 2-3 small dates to replace 1 Tbsp. of honey. You can soak the dates first in water for one or two hours to make them easier to mix with the other ingredients.

Jalapeño pepper — Pronounce, "Ha-la-pee-nio." A hot variety of pepper, used in small quantities to spice dishes, and very popular in Mexican cuisine. It is sold fresh. Available green and red.

Miso — Miso is a fermented product made out of soybeans. It is used in Asian cuisine, and comes in many flavors, my favorite being the mellow white miso. Buy it unpasteurized. You can find this in health food stores. It is not a totally "raw" product, since the soybeans are cooked. But after the long fermentation—a transformative enzymatic process—it is considered to be "living."

Nama Shoyu, or Tamari sauce — Nama Shoyu is a tasty soy sauce that is unpasteurized. While not being entirely raw (some cooked ingredients are used in the process), it can still be considered a living food, as it is rich in enzymes created during the fermentation process. If you do not find Nama Shoyu at your local health food store, you can buy "tamari sauce," which is a pasteurized version similar in taste. You may also order Nama Shoyu by mail order.

Olive oil — Purchase olive oil that is organic and cold pressed. The very best olive oil is "stone-pressed." Stone-pressed olive oil has been pressed using the ancient method of the Greeks. It has a very rich, fruity flavor, and is much more nutritious, due to the care taken at every step of the oil production process.

Pickled Ginger — Strips of peeled ginger that have been marinated in vinegar and sea salt. Can be found in most health food stores, near the sea vegetable section.

Sea salt — Sea salt should be bought totally unrefined. The best unrefined sea salt is sold under the name of "Celtic Sea Salt" in the health food stores. It often comes from France. But it can also be sold under other names. Good quality sea salt should still be slightly moist. You can buy it "coarse" or "fine." "Coarse" sea salt comes in bigger pieces, while "fine" sea salt looks more like regular table salt. I usually use the "coarse" variety, but most people prefer the "fine" variety for its ease of use.

Spirulina flakes — Spirulina is a form of edible algae usually sold as a food supplement, because of its extreme richness in protein, vitamins, minerals, and other nutrients. But it is really a food, and can be used as a regular item on the table. Spirulina is usually sold either in capsules, or in a powdered form. This type of Spirulina is not usually very tasty. But I have found a very good type of Spirulina, sold in flake form, with added lecithin. It is very tasty, and has a nice, salty quality.

Sun-dried olives — These are dried, black olives preserved in olive oil and sea salt. Sun-dried olives may be added to salads, or eaten on their own. To remove excess salt from the olives, you may soak them for a few days in water, changing the water twice a day.

Sun-dried tomatoes — Sun-dried tomatoes are often sold soaking in olive oil, but also plain in packages, or in bulk. We recommend the organic, sun-dried tomato halves, sold in bulk. Make sure they do not have any salt or chemical preservatives added. Even better, make your own sun-dried tomatoes during the tomato season, using a food dehydrator. To use sun-dried tomatoes for a recipe, soak them first in water for at least one hour. The longer they soak, the softer they will be. You can soak them up to 24 hours.

Tahini — This is a rich paste made out of hulled sesame seeds. Buy it raw and organic. Because of its great flavor, consistency, and nutritional value, tahini is commonly used in **The Sunfood Cuisine**.

Vanilla extract — Natural vanilla extract can be used to enhance the flavor of living desserts. Buy it without alcohol from the health food store.

Wild rice — Wild rice is not a true grain, but a seed. It is in fact not at all related to rice, but named that way because of its appearance. Wild rice grows in Canada and the northern United States, and is still harvested from the wild. It is a really nutritious and hearty addition to **The Sunfood Cuisine**. Wild rice may be eaten raw, but has to be sprouted beforehand. Soak a cup or two of wild rice for 24 hours in a jar. Then drain the water, and rinse two times a day for the next two or three days until the rice is soft enough to eat. It usually takes 2 or 3 days of sprouting (plus one day of soaking). I like to soak wild rice in a large, glass container, and then place it in a large strainer, the same type that is used to drain pasta. It is then easy to run water over it twice a day. Place the strainer full of wild rice in a bowl, to avoid getting water everywhere. You may then make delicious salads with the wild rice, or add it to other dishes.

Young coconut meat — The tender flesh of a coconut that has been picked before maturity. You may find these young white "Thai" coconuts in many Asian markets.

Coconut palms growing in paradise

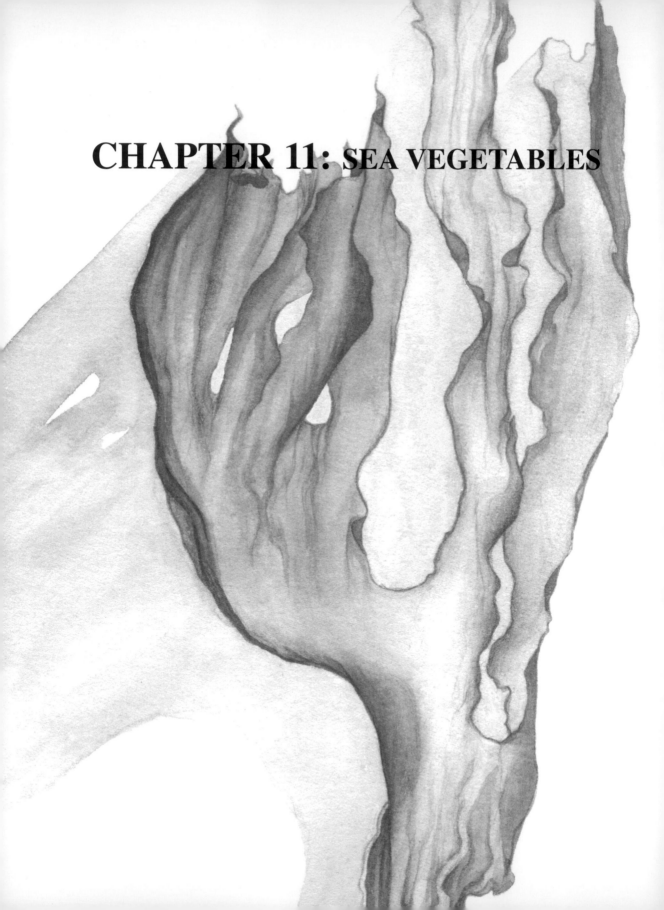

CHAPTER 11: SEA VEGETABLES

Sea vegetables are an important part of **The Sunfood Cuisine**. My friend, John Ferney, M.D., who is a big advocate of sea vegetables, says, "There are about one hundred minerals and trace minerals in the ocean. Human blood contains them all, and you must replace them on a regular basis. Seaweed is the way to bring these minerals into our diet, as they are integrated into the plant in a most assimilable form." Vegetables and fruits grown on large farms are becoming less reliable as good sources for minerals, as erosion and overfarming is creating poorer and poorer soil. Sea vegetables are wild plants that contain all the minerals that we need.

Arame — Similar to hijiki, but with a milder taste. It is harvested in Japan, and the Pacific North American coast. Arame has to be soaked 10 minutes before being used. It is a good source of iron, calcium, and iodine.

Dulse — This is our favorite sea vegetable. Dulse can be bought whole leaf or in flakes. We generally rinse whole leaf dulse for a few seconds, making it more tender and easier to cut. You can eat dulse on its own as a snack, or add it to salads, soups, and dips. It is an excellent source of iron and iodine. Seaweeds should be kept in a cool, dry place — preferably in a glass container.

Hijiki — This is a mild sea vegetable that has to be soaked for about 10 minutes before being used. It will quadruple in size as it soaks. It is rich in calcium and iron.

Kelp — The most common seaweed, kelp, is usually used in **The Sunfood Cuisine** in a powdered form. It is rich in minerals, and powdered kelp can be used in place of salt.

Nori — Nori is a popular seaweed that comes in thin sheets. These are used to make sushi or Nori rolls **(see page 204)**. The toasted Nori is greenish in appearance, while the sun-dried kind is black. Nori is rich in quality-protein, and in vitamins A, B1, and B3.

Wakame — A brown seaweed that grows in long, thin strips. Like hijiki, wakame should also be soaked before being used.

CHAPTER 12: THE EQUIPMENT

In **The Sunfood Cuisine**, there are many things you will not need: stoves, microwaves, toasters, and other machines that heat food. Many of the tools you are familiar with, and may already have in your kitchen, are used in the preparation of **The Sunfood Cuisine**.

COMMON TOOLS THAT ARE USED IN THE SUNFOOD CUISINE

Bowls • Cutting board • Funnel • Grater • Measuring cups • Pie server

Pie tins • Plates • Set of knives • Strainer • Vegetable peeler

Other tools, such as blenders, food processors, juicers, and dehydrators are also very useful. You will not need all of these tools in order to make most of the recipes in this book, but many of the tools, such as the Vita-Mix blender, are so versatile and useful that we use them on a daily basis. Remember that money invested in these tools is an investment in your health.

BLENDER — One of the most common and useful kitchen appliances is a blender. A blender liquefies foods, thus providing us with maximum nutrients, with less work needing to be done by the digestive system.

Your choice of a blender will determine the quality of your blended meals. Using low-end blenders for blending hard vegetables and leafy greens will be difficult, if not impossible — or, at least, very messy. You will need a good commercial type blender to do this. I have found the "Vita-Mix" to be the best blender. You will have to make sure that whatever model you purchase has a strong motor, and the capacity to blend a lot more than a typical blender. Try to get a heavy-duty blender that can hold twice as much as a regular blender.

VITA-MIX — The Vita-Mix (or a heavy-duty blender) is one of the most important tools you can use in your raw-vegan kitchen. So what is so great about this machine? Well, first of all, the Vita-Mix is more than a blender. True, it is a heavy-duty blender, but it does more than any typical, cheap blender. It can contain twice as much as a regular blender, and its heavy-duty motor can blend basically anything you put in there into a fine liquid. It is a powerful machine!

So what can you use the Vita-Mix for? Mostly, you will use it in the preparation of raw soups, smoothies, nut milks, and pâtés. But you can also use it to grind nuts, and chop vegetables — although a food processor might be more appropriate for that type of job. Basically you will use the Vita-Mix to turn foods into a liquid. As we do a lot of blending in **The Sunfood Cuisine**, you will want something that totally blends, with almost no visible particles left. The Vita-Mix is suited for this.

CHAMPION JUICER—The Champion is another popular machine used in preparing **The Sunfood Cuisine**. It is a mastication juicer that can juice soft fruits with ease, and is also used as a food processor. It can turn nuts into nut butters, or frozen fruit into ice cream. We use it to make all of our nut pâtés, and to make juice. It is fast and easy to clean. The downsides are that it cannot juice green vegetables very well, and tends to heat up the foods. Also, it cannot properly juice celery and other tough and fibrous vegetables.

GREEN POWER/GREEN LIFE JUICER—The Green Power Juicer is a step up from the Champion Juicer. It has been specifically designed to juice green vegetables. The Green Power Juicer uses twin gears, which crush the foods at a slow pace. It extracts the most out of fruits and vegetables, without heating them, thus preserving all of the enzymes and trace minerals. It also makes ice cream out of frozen fruits as well as nut butters just like the Champion. The downsides are that it is not the best juicer to juice fruits and it takes a little longer to clean. It remains our juicer of choice nonetheless. The Green Life juicer is very similar to the Green Power, made by the same company. It misses a few features, such as pasta making that you may not use anyway.

OTHER TYPES OF JUICERS—There are many types of juicers on the market that could be very useful in preparing **The Sunfood Cuisine**. We will not discuss all of them in this book because we believe that the two juicers described earlier are the best investments one could make for the kitchen— and one's health.

DEHYDRATOR—The dehydrator is another popular tool used by many Sunfoodists. With a dehydrator, you can dehydrate fruits and vegetables to preserve them, and also make delicious crackers, cookies, and other treats. The dehydrator could be considered the "oven" of **The Sunfood Cuisine**. It is important to use the dehydrator at a low heat so as to preserve the nutrients.

The dehydrator is an optional tool that is great to have, but not necessary. I realize that most people do not have a dehydrator. Because of this, I have separated out the few recipes in this book that need dehydration and placed them in a special section at the end of chapter 24. In case you are considering buying a dehydrator, the best brand on the market is the Excalibur dehydrator. It comes with 4, 5, or 9 trays. I recommend getting either the 5 or 9 tray model, because they include a fan to regulate the temperature. If you buy a dehydrator, you will also need "Teflex" sheets, which are reusable plastic-like sheets that allow you to dehydrate wet/moist ingredients such as: crackers, crusts and other raw food recipes.

OTHER TOOLS USED

COFFEE GRINDER—The coffee grinder is used in **The Sunfood Cuisine** to grind flax seeds, sesame seeds, and other seeds and small nuts. It's an inexpensive and useful tool to have.

FOOD PROCESSOR—Food processors still have their role in the kitchen, even if you already have the other tools described. Food processors are ideal for making crusts for living pies, for making date paste, and for grating cabbage and other vegetables.

SALADACCO—The Saladacco, also called the Spiralizer, is a little machine that we love. It turns vegetables like zucchinis, carrots, beets, and other hard vegetables into pasta-like strips. We use it to make garnishing for various dishes. It is a very fun tool that I think everyone should acquire.

CITRUS JUICER—Citrus juicers are usually inexpensive, and nice to have handy when making orange juice or other citrus juices. You can get a fairly good electric citrus juicer for less than $20.

PART 3:
THE SUNFOOD RECIPES

ABBREVIATIONS AND EXPRESSIONS USED IN THE RECIPES

Tbsp. —Tablespoon (level)

tsp. —Teaspoon (level)

Diced — Chopped finely

Pitted — With pit removed

Minced — Cut small with a knife

Shredded — Shredded either with a hand shredder or food processor

Soaked Raisins (or other dried fruit) — Raisins or fruit that have been covered with water in a bowl for an hour or two.

Soaked sunflower seeds (or almonds, sesame seeds, etc.) — Seeds that have been previously soaked. Refers to the quantity of the nuts or seeds after they have been soaked. To get 2 cups of soaked nuts or seeds, you will have to soak approximately 1 to 1 1/2 cups of nuts or seeds for 8 to 12 hours.

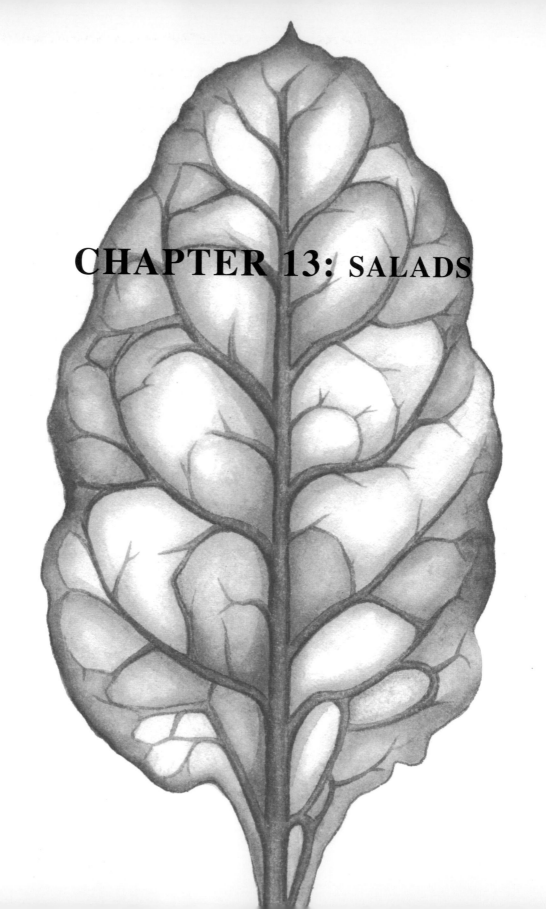

CHAPTER 13: SALADS

The salad is often viewed as the primary staple of a healthy diet. Everyone needs to eat more green vegetables, and salads are a perfect way to eat more of these important foods. Green vegetables are an important source of minerals, especially calcium, which is essential for maintaining health.

A couple years ago there was a turning point in my salad making abilities. In the beginning I made fairly good salads, but nothing to be excited about. Somehow, I learned how to make salads that brought a lot of positive comments. Because of the praise I was receiving from those who ate my salads, I decided to stop and analyze what I was doing. I asked myself such questions as: "What is so different about my salads?" "How come when I go to a restaurant they always serve me a salad that is less than amazing, no matter how good the restaurant is?" and "What is the process I go through in order to create a perfect salad every time?" After all, I didn't use any recipes; I just used whatever was in the refrigerator at the moment. I threw together a bunch of stuff in a bowl, and some magic seemed to occur that no one seemed to be able to reproduce. I thought I had a special talent like some magician or fortune-teller. But that was far from the truth. I was just an ordinary man, with a technique that operated from the level of the subconscious. I would make good salads because I used the same process everytime.

The key to making amazing food is understanding how to combine different flavors that you normally would not think of mixing together. So what are those basic flavors?

Sweet
Sour
Salty
Bitter

That is what you learned in school, remember? But there is a lot more to it than that. There are many different textures that you can to play with too! Here are some other flavors, textures, and taste sensations that are important:

Juicy
Fatty
Creamy
Hot (spicy)
Tangy
Fruity
Crunchy
Crispy

Here is what I came up with: every time I made a salad, I would use certain categories of ingredients that possessed some of the textures or flavors I just mentioned, and found original ways to include these flavors in my salads.

I also found that the categories of food I often mixed together were of the following combinations:

Crunchy-Bitter — Green vegetables
Tangy-Sour — Lemon juice, or apple cider vinegar
Fatty-Creamy — Avocado, oil, or nut butters
Salty — Sea salt, sea vegetables, Nama Shoyu, or tamari sauce
Sweet — Fruits, sweet nuts, or honey

I often used **spicy ingredients**, such as: garlic, onion, or cayenne pepper.

Also, I realized that there were two basic rules I followed when making a salad. One is to make the dressing separately, and add it on top of the salad. The dressing then contains some of the previously listed flavors in it, and is poured onto a variety of greens. The other is to simply add the dressing ingredients directly into the salad by mixing all of the ingredients together in a bowl.

Once I came to the realization that this was the process I used to create great salads, I went out and taught it to some of my friends. They soon became great salad makers, without any recipes. Sometimes after I made them a salad they asked me, "So where's the sweet ingredient?" and I responded: "There's no sweet ingredient in that salad." They were surprised that I did not follow my own rules. Then I explained to them that the rules are not strict rules, but general guidelines that did not have to be followed to the letter. They are simply ideas to be played with.

Using the following chart, you can make perfect salads, without having to follow any recipes. Or you may also try out my salad recipes, or salad and dressing recipes, and find out for yourself how I apply some of these concepts in the creation of a salad.

To make a perfect salad, learn to combine ingredients from each of the following categories in an original way. Remember that your salads do not need to contain all of the ingredients. Let one flavor dominate.

Vegetables and Greens

Asparagus
Chard
Chopped broccoli
Chopped cauliflower
Collards
Curly lettuce
Kale
Parsley
Purple or white cabbage
Romaine lettuce
Slices of cucumber
Slices of mushrooms
Spinach
Strips of multi-colored peppers
Zucchini
All other vegetables

Tangy-Sour Flavorings or Ingredients

Apple cider vinegar
Lemon juice
Lime juice
Passion fruit juice
Pomegranate seeds
Pomegranate juice
Sorrel
Sourgrass
Tomatoes

Oily-Fatty Flavorings or Ingredients

Avocado
Flax seed oil, olive oil, hemp oil (Always used the cold pressed-varieties)
Ground nuts and seeds
Tahini
Whole soaked nuts and/or seeds

SALAD RECIPES

Venice

2 cups **mixed greens** (young spinach, arugula, etc.)
1 head **lettuce**, chopped
1 **tomato**, diced
1 cup **arugula**, chopped
10-20 **kalamata olives**, pitted and chopped
1 **avocado**, peeled and diced
4 Tbsp. **olive oil**
2 Tbsp. **nama shoyu**, or tamari sauce
1 **lime** or **lemon**, juice of
1 handful **pine nuts**

Mix all of the vegetables in a bowl, along with the olives and avocado. Drizzle with olive oil, nama shoyu or tamari sauce, lime or lemon juice, and sprinkle with pine nuts. Pine nuts are sweet and creamy, and add richness to this salad.

If you cannot find kalamata olives, you can use other types of olives, but it is not recommended to use "sun-dried" olives in this recipe, as they are too bitter for this type of salad. Serves 3-4.

Coucher de Soleil

8 cups **lettuce** (any kind you like), chopped
2 cups **purple cabbage**, minced
1 cup **parsley**, finely chopped
2 **avocados**, peeled and diced
2 Tbsp. **flax seed oil**, or olive oil
1 **lime** or **lemon**, juice of
2 Tbsp. **apple cider vinegar**
1 Tbsp. **honey** diluted in 1 Tbsp. water
pinch of **sea salt**
dash of **nama shoyu,** or tamari sauce

Mix all of the ingredients in a bowl. Or, you can also start by mixing the last 7 ingredients in a bowl first, and then add the remaining ingredients. Serves 3-5.

Olive Lover

1 head **romaine** lettuce, chopped
1 1/2 cups **purple cabbage**, shredded or finely chopped
1 cup **arugula**, chopped
15-20 **sun-dried black olives**, pitted and chopped

Chop the lettuce, or tear it with your hands. Place in a bowl. Shred, finely chop or mince the cabbage. You may use a food processor to do this. Mix the first three ingredients in a bowl. Sprinkle olives on top. Serve with Mild Avocado-Olive Oil Dressing **(page 126)**, or simply with olive oil, lemon juice (or apple cider vinegar), and a dash of sea salt. Serves 3-4.

Caesar

1 head **romaine lettuce**
1 cup **parsley**, chopped
1 cup **arugula**, chopped
2 cups **tomato**, diced
3-4 **red radishes**, sliced thinly
3-4 **white mushrooms**, sliced

Mix all of the ingredients in a bowl. Decorate with sliced mushrooms and radishes. Serve with The House's Favorite Dressing **(page 126)**. Serves 3-4.

Fast Service

6 cups of your favorite varieties of **lettuces** and **greens**, chopped
1/4 cup **onion**, diced
1 cup **tomato**, diced
1/2 **yellow bell pepper**, or red bell pepper, cut into strips
1/2 **cucumber**, sliced

Place artistically in a bowl. Serve with one of the dressings in **Chapter 14.** Serves 2-4.

Cole Slaw

4 cups **white cabbage**, shredded
2 cups **carrots**, shredded
1/2 **red bell pepper**, diced
1 1/2 cups **avocado mayonnaise (page 193)**
1 pinch **black pepper** (optional)

Mix all ingredients in a bowl. Sprinkle with black pepper if desired. Serve with flax crackers. Serves 2-4.

Frédéric's Favorite Salad

2 cups **mixed greens** (preferably baby greens)
1/2 **head romaine** or frisée lettuce, chopped
1 cup **arugula**, chopped
2 medium **tomatoes**, diced
1 large **avocado**, peeled and diced
1 **lime** or **lemon**, juice of
1 handful **whole leaf dulse**
3-4 Tbsp. **olive oil**
1 **pinch sea salt** (optional)

Mix all of the greens in a bowl with the tomatoes. Add lime juice and olive oil on top. Dice the avocado and mash on top. Rinse the dulse briefly, cut and arrange nicely around the salad. Sprinkle with a little sea salt if desired. Serves 2-3.

Mustard Salad

2-3 cups ****organic greens** mix
1/2 **head romaine lettuce**, chopped
1-2 **leaves mustard greens**
1 **cucumber**, diced
1-2 **avocados**, peeled and diced
2 **limes** or 1 big lemon, juice of
1 handful **whole leaf dulse**, rinsed briefly and chopped
3-4 Tbsp. **flax seed oil**, or other cold-pressed oil

Mix all ingredients in a bowl.

** Organic baby greens mix is found in health food stores, and sometimes in supermarkets. If not available, combine greens, such as mustard and dandelion, with other greens such as your favorite type of lettuce. Or, for a new experience, gather edible weeds from your yard and use them.

Arizona Winter

1/4 cup **olive oil**
1/4 cup **grapefruit juice**
1/2 tsp. **sea salt**
2 Tbsp. **nama shoyu**, or tamari sauce
1 Tbsp. **dried sage**
1 Tbsp. **dried mint**
1/4 tsp. **cayenne pepper**
4 cups **chard**, chopped
4 cups **lettuce**, chopped
2 cups **kale**, chopped
2 cups **spinach**, chopped

In a large bowl, stir the olive oil, grapefruit juice, salt, nama shoyu, sage, mint, and cayenne pepper together. Add the remaining ingredients. Mix well. Use more or less olive oil depending on your taste. This is an example of how you can use the sweet taste of a fruit (grapefruit) to balance the rest of the ingredients. Serves 3-5.

Crisp and Green

1 head **romaine lettuce**, chopped
2 cups **kale**, chopped
2 cups ****lettuce mix**
5-7 red **radishes**, sliced
1 **cucumber**, sliced
2 **apples**, peeled and diced

Mix all ingredients together in a bowl. The apples in this recipe add a refreshing element. Serve with Eden Dressing **(page 128)**.

**Lettuce mix may be found in all good health food stores. It is also called "Baby Greens Mix" or "Spring Mix."

Sprout Salad

6 cups **clover** or alfalfa sprouts
your favorite dressing

Place sprouts in a bowl. Soak with your favorite dressing.

CHAPTER 14: DRESSINGS

Many people cannot imagine salad without dressing. Dressings are meant to enhance the flavor of a salad. In **The Sunfood Cuisine**, dressings are highly nutritious. These nutritious dressings balance the green leafy vegetables, which form the base of the salads, to turn them into complete, satisfying meals.

The typical commercial dressing sold in most stores contains the following main ingredients: fat (in the form of low quality oil), sugar (usually corn syrup or another artificial sweetener), salt (processed, heated table salt), and vinegar. These dressings are flavored with spices and artificial agents, and contain preservatives that make these factory-made concoctions very unhealthy.

Regardless of ingredients, many people like the taste of store-bought dressings. While there are organic dressings that you may purchase at your health food store, not all of these products are completely healthy. Many contain low-quality oil. It is possible, using your blender or Vita-Mix, to create super-tasty dressings that will taste much better than any store-bought dressing!

THE BASIC INGREDIENTS IN A DRESSING

OIL — Oil is often the most important part of a dressing. It adds body and flavor to both the dressing and the salad. Although oil is important, you can also achieve a rich consistency with little oil, a point that might be important for people trying to cut down on fat.

TANGY — Vinegar is used in many salad dressings. In **The Sunfood Cuisine** we may use apple cider vinegar, which is raw, and also lime juice, or lemon juice, to give a tangy bite. The dressing may also be blended with other fruit juices, such as orange juice, or with tomatoes, for an additional tangy effect.

SUGAR — SWEET — In traditional dressings, some sort of sweetener is always used. In **The Sunfood Cuisine**, when we choose to sweeten our dressings, we use the natural sweetness of fruit. Fruit sugar in dressing adds a really nice flavor that most people appreciate. However, it is not necessary to use sweet elements in dressings.

SALT — It is good to make dressings as savory as possible. We usually add sea salt, nama shoyu (or tamari sauce), or sea vegetables, to enhance the flavor.

SPICES — HERBS — Beside the items listed above, spices may also be used to enhance the flavor of salads. Experiment with your favorite herbs in dressing recipes to find flavor combinations that are the most pleasing to you.

BODY INGREDIENTS —The previous categories of ingredients are rather strong tasting, so we like to blend our dressings with vegetables to add body without having to use too much fat. We like to use non-sweet fruits, such as cucumbers and tomatoes, as a dressing base. We may also add water.

To create a basic dressing, choose ingredients from each of the following categories, and blend them together. Find an original way to mix the flavors that taste pleasant to you.

Oily Ingredients

Almond butter
Avocado
Cold-pressed flax seed oil
Cold-pressed hemp seed oil
Extra-virgin olive oil
Nut butters
Soaked almonds
Soaked sunflower seeds
Other soaked nuts or seeds
Tahini
Young coconut meat
Other cold-pressed oil, such as sunflower oil

Kirlian Field of
olive oil (on the left) and lard (on the right)

Tangy-Sour Flavoring

Apple cider vinegar
Lemon juice
Lime juice
Orange juice (also counts as sweet)
Tangerine juice (also counts as sweet)
Passion fruit juice (also counts as sweet)
Other fruit juice (also counts as sweet)
Tomatoes

Sweet Flavorings or Ingredients (optional)

Dates and/or other dried fruit
Honey
Orange juice (also counts as tangy)
Tangerine juice (also counts as tangy)
Passion fruit juice (also counts as tangy)
Other fruit juice (also counts as tangy)
Fresh fruits such as mango, pear, or persimmon

Salty Flavorings or Ingredients

Celery
Sea salt
Dulse, in flakes or whole
Kelp powder
Nama shoyu, or tamari sauce

Spices and Herbs

Cayenne pepper
Jalapeño pepper
Garlic
Ginger
Herbs, such as dill, thyme, rosemary, oregano, or basil
Onion — red, white, Spanish, or shallots
Spices, such as curry or black pepper

Body Ingredients

Carrots
Celery
Cucumber
Tomato
Zucchini

How long can you keep these dressings? Many of the following dressings, as they contain fresh ingredients, will only keep for a couple days in the refrigerator. I would suggest that you adjust the quantities to fit your needs.

DRESSING RECIPES

Tomato-Tahini

2 medium **tomatoes**
2 **lemons**, juice of
1/4 cup **olive oil**
1/4 cup **tahini**
3 Tbsp. **nama shoyu**, or tamari sauce
1/2 tsp. **sea salt**
1 tsp. **cumin,** (or basil, dill, oregano)

Blend. If you have fresh herbs use them, but triple or quadruple the quantity. This dressing is great served over a bed of greens.

The House's Favorite Dressing

2 **avocados**
1/4 cup **olive oil**
1/4 cup **tahini**
2/3 cup **water**
2 Tbsp. **apple cider vinegar**
1 **lemon**, juice of
2-4 Tbsp. **nama shoyu**, or tamari (to taste)
1 pinch **cayenne pepper**
1 tsp. (choose one): ** **dried paprika**, **dried dill**, **curry**, or **dried basil**.

Blend. Add some more water if needed, or desired.

**Change the herb every time you make the dressing. When using fresh dill or basil, you can quadruple the amount.

Mild Avocado—Olive Oil Dressing

2 **avocados**
1 **tomato**
1/4 cup **olive oil**
2 **limes** or small lemon, juice of
1/2 tsp. **sea salt**
1 tsp. **Italian herb** mix (a mix of basil, thyme, oregano, and garlic)

Blend. Add water if needed.

Better Than Ranch Dressing

1 cup **tomato**
1 cup **young coconut meat**
1/4 cup **olive oil**
1/4 cup **apple cider vinegar**
1 Tbsp. **mellow miso**
1/2 tsp. **sea salt**
1 Tbs. ****dried dill**
1 pinch **cayenne pepper**

> Blend. Add water if necessary. This is better than Ranch Dressing!
> **If using fresh dill quadruple the amount.

Curry Dressing

1/2 cup **olive oil**
1 **lemon**, juice of
2 Tbsp. **tahini**
1 Tbsp. **honey**, or 2-3 pitted dates
1 tsp. **curry powder**
1 **garlic clove**
1 inch of **fresh ginger**
1/3 cup **water**
1/2 tsp. **sea salt** (optional)

> Blend and serve.

Parsley Dressing

4 cups **parsley** (one bunch)
2 cups **water**
2-4 Tbsp. **nama shoyu**, or tamari sauce (to taste)
1 **avocado**
2 Tbsp. **tahini**
1 **lemon**, juice of
3 Tbsp. **apple cider vinegar**
1/2 tsp. **sea salt**
1 pinch of **cayenne pepper**
4-5 pitted **dates**

> Blend. If you feel you need to eat more greens, this dressing served over a green salad will be a good way to get started. When you feel ready for it, move to the <u>Green-Green Dressing</u>, **page 129**.

Good and Simple

2 cups **sunflower seeds**, soaked overnight
4 Tbsp. **lemon juice**
1 tsp. to 1 1/2 tsp. **sea salt**
2/3 cup **olive oil**
1 cup **water**
1 pinch **cayenne pepper**
2 tsp. **curry powder**

　　Blend. This is a rich dressing to use in moderation.

Eden Dressing

2 cups soaked ****cashews**
1/2 cup **water**
4 Tbsp. **nama shoyu**, or tamari sauce
1/2 tsp. **sea salt**
4 Tbsp. **lemon** or lime juice
2 cups **cucumber** or tomatoes, diced

　　Blend.

　　**The cashews should be soaked overnight.

Sunburst Dressing

1 cup **orange juice**
1/2 cup **water**
2 cups soaked **sunflower seeds**
4 **green onions**
2 **lemons**, juice of
8 Tbsp. **almond butter**
1-2 tsp. **sea salt** (to taste)
1 pinch **cayenne pepper**
2 tsp. **curry powder**

　　Blend.

Italian Dressing

1 cup **olive oil**
1 1/2 cups **tomatoes**
6 Tbsp. **apple cider vinegar**
3-4 Tbsp. **nama shoyu**, or tamari sauce (to taste)
2 Tbsp. **honey**
2 tsp. **Italian herb mix** (a mix of basil, thyme, oregano, and garlic)
1 **garlic clove**

Blend.

Thai Dressing

1 cup **water**
1 inch **fresh ginger**
6 Tbsp. **tahini**
3 Tbsp. ****unpasteurized miso**
1 **lemon**, juice of

Blend.

**Any kind of unpasteurized miso works for this recipe.

Green-Green Dressing

2 cups **kale**
1 cup **arugula**, cilantro, or parsley
1 **avocado**
2 cups **water**
2 **limes**, juice of
4 Tbsp. **olive oil**
1 cup dulse
1/2 - 1 tsp. **sea salt** (to taste)

Blend. Serve over a green salad. This recipe is very healing and might not be appropriate for beginners. It one of my favorites. I find it to be a perfect winter food, anti-depressant, and alkalinizing remedy.

Smooth Carrot

2 cups **carrots**, diced
1 cup **water**
1/4 cup **apple cider vinegar**
1/4 cup **tahini**
1 tsp. **honey**, or 2 pitted dates
1 tsp. **sea salt**
1 tsp. **paprika**

    Blend.

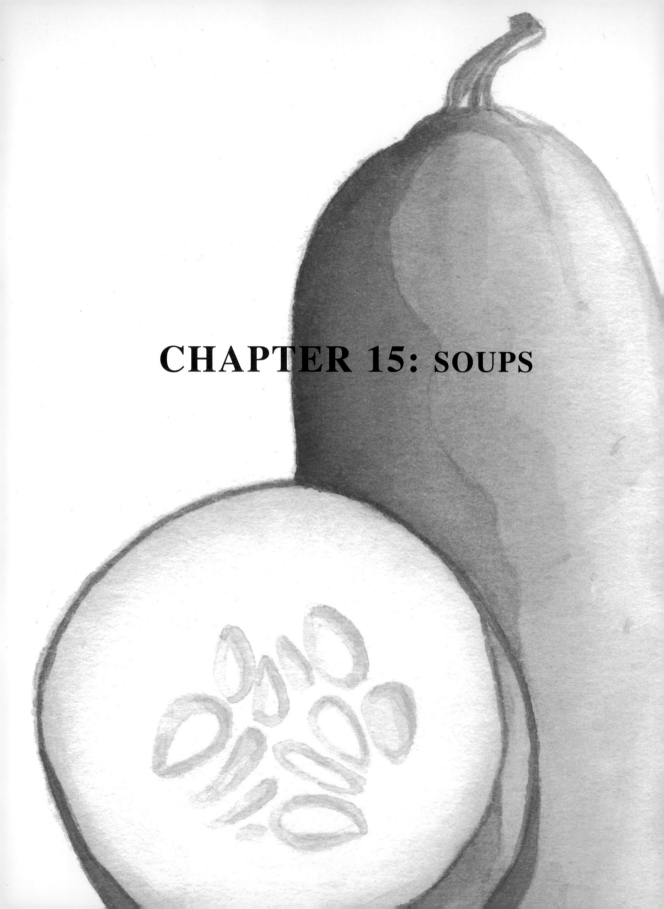

CHAPTER 15: SOUPS

THE ADVANTAGES OF BLENDED FOODS

Ease of digestion
The whole purpose of the digestive process is to turn the foods you eat into a liquid, so that the nutrients may be transported into the cells of the body. Most people do not chew long enough, and therefore they do not get full nutritional value out of the foods they eat. Someone once said: "Chew your food well for the stomach has no teeth." The advantage of blended food is that it has already been transformed into a liquid. This does not mean that you should not eat whole foods, and learn to chew well, but it helps you add some truly assimilable foods to your diet.

Cleansing effect
Blended foods are very cleansing. Since blended foods pass through the system very fast, and do not require much energy for their assimilation, the body can use the leftover energy to detoxify. When you eat only blended foods for a few days, it is a great relief for your digestive organs. They can rest for a little while and take out some of the "garbage" that has been sitting around. Eating only blended foods a few days each month is a good practice to build great health.

Time saving
Many people feel they do not have time to eat correctly. For instance, we all know that we should be eating salads and leafy greens everyday, but how many of us really do? Using your Vita-Mix or blender, you can make delicious soups and smoothies in only a few minutes. It also takes a lot less time to eat all these vegetables or fruits in a blended form than if you had to sit down and chew every single one of them.

Assimilation
Most people do not experience perfect digestion. Although they may be eating large amounts of food, most of it remains undigested. Blending is a wonderful solution to this problem. Blended foods are easily assimilable, as they already have been transformed into a liquid.

THE BLENDED FOOD FAST

Many people try to fast on juice or water in order to improve their health. For many of them, it soon proves to be too difficult in their environment, with their work and obligations. A good alternative to fasting on juice or water is to try the "nutritional fast," where you can drink juices and have blended foods. You will get all the nutrition you need, and also the benefits of a fast, but with more energy and less cleansing reactions. When doing a "nutritional fast," try to have raw soups everyday. This way you will get the nutrition and fiber that you need to keep you going.

HOW TO MAKE GREAT LIVING SOUPS

Raw soups are one of my favorite dishes. I have gone weeks eating nothing but various raw soups, juices, and smoothies that I have made in my Vita-Mix. I especially enjoy soups because they are easy to make, are tasty, easy to digest, and give my body a digestive rest.

The typical living soup consists of vegetables blended with some liquid, creamed with some fatty ingredients — such as avocado, oil, or nut butter — and flavored with something savory and salty. To make soup heartier, you may also stir in some spirulina flakes, avocado pieces, or diced vegetables. I found that in making a typical soup, I blend together the following:

Non-Sweet Fruit — I like to use about two to three cups of non-sweet fruit, such as tomato, zucchini, cucumber, or pepper. Why? Because these foods are high in water, have little fiber, and when blended turn into a liquid. They form a good soup base.

Greens — I often blend kale, spinach, parsley, and other vegetables into soup to give it both taste and a nutritional boost. Depending on the bitterness of the vegetables, I may add anywhere from one to two cups of them. I always try to make sure my soups are not too bitter. A salad is different, and you may get by with some bitterness. But, because the soups are liquid, and more apt to cling to the palate, they are less than excellent if they have a strong bitter taste. With bitter vegetables such as kale, I may use only one cup but I may use more of the non-bitter vegetables, such as spinach. Besides green vegetables, you may also blend in some hard vegetables that will add a thicker consistency to the soup such as: carrots, broccoli, or sunchokes.

Since there is a limit to what can fit into a blender, choose only one or two ingredients out of the greens category. Remember that soups do not always have to be "everything but the kitchen sink." It is sometimes good to let one flavor dominate, whether it be a vegetable, a spice, or a fruit. Simple can be better, and fewer flavors may provide a better taste.

Liquid —The need for adding additional liquid into raw soups depends on the quantity of non-sweet fruits being used. Most of the time I add one or two cups of liquids. Distilled water, coconut water, or vegetable juices are the most common liquids I use.

Fatty Ingredients — I like soups to be filling and hearty. But even when making light soups, I may use something to provide creaminess. For this I often use two or three types of fatty ingredients. These may include: avocado, young coconut meat, tahini, nut butter, ground seeds, olive oil, cold-pressed flax seed oil, or miso. **Choose one to three of the following:**

- 1/2 to one avocado
- meat of one or two young coconuts
- 4 Tbsp. tahini or other nut butter
- 1/2 cup ground seeds, such as pumpkin or sunflower
- 1/8 to 1/4 cup oil, such as olive oil, hemp oil, or flax seed oil
- 2 Tbsp. miso

Sweet Ingredients — Soups may vary from sweet to salty to spicy. Sometimes they may be a combination of all these. Occasionally, I choose coconut water for a liquid, which is sweet. In addition to, or in place of, the coconut water, I may add one-half to one apple, or another type of fruit, such as mango, a little honey, or some miso. Miso counts as both a fatty ingredient and salty ingredient. Adding sweetness to a soup is an art in itself. It is easy to put too much sweetness into a soup, and this may make it taste more like some type of smoothie than a dinner soup.

Salty-Savory Ingredient — It is really important to make soups taste savory. I often choose sea salt over any other salty ingredients, but I also like to use miso, nama shoyu (or tamari sauce), and sometimes a sea vegetable such as kelp or dulse.

Spicy Ingredient — It is good to use more spices in a soup than you would in a salad. Why? Because soups are usually eaten warm, and give you that feeling of comfort as they heat your internal organs. With a cold soup, it is hard to achieve the same thing — unless you add some spice. My spices of choice for soup include: garlic, onion, ginger, cayenne pepper, curry powder, or chili peppers (but not all at the same time). The garlic-chili flax seed oil is great way to add both oil and spice at the same time.

The following is the Basic Soup Recipe, which uses ingredients from all of the categories I have listed.

Basic Soup Recipe

2 cups **non-sweet fruit**
> Choose between cucumber, tomato, zucchini, pepper, or tomatillo. You
> may choose one or more of these.

1 to 2 cups **liquid**
> Use one cup first. Then, if needed, add more liquid at the end.
> Choose between distilled water, coconut water, or vegetable juice.

1 to 2 cups **greens**
> Vegetables or herbs. Choose between kale, parsley, spinach, arugula
> (also a spice), celery, carrots, cilantro, and your favorite herbs and
> vegetables.

1/2 to 1 **avocado**, meat of one young coconut, or 2-4 Tbsp. of tahini

4 Tbsp. **olive oil**, or other cold pressed oil

2 Tbsp. **miso**

1/2 **apple**

1/2 tsp. **sea salt**, or 2 Tbsp. nama shoyu (or tamari sauce)

1 inch **ginger**

1 **garlic clove**

1 pinch **cayenne pepper**

> Blend all ingredients. You may also create a chunky soup by dicing some of
> the vegetables, and adding them into the ones that you have blended.

This soup is a basic recipe. It is easy to prepare, and tasty. But, as you will see
by trying the soup recipes listed, I do not always follow my own rules — they
are just general guidelines rather than inflexible rules.

Another way to make the soup is to use vegetable juice as a base. Carrot juice
works well for this. Creaminess may be added by blending some avocado or
tahini. Flavorings may be added by adding nama shoyu or sea salt, and spices
such as ginger, cayenne pepper, and curry. This technique of making a base is
one that I know, but rarely do. Just the idea of spending all the time juicing and
cleaning the juicer does not appeal to me. If I juice, then I am likely to enjoy
the juice as a meal.

Remember that it is sometimes good to let one flavor dominate. If you make a
cilantro soup, it should taste like cilantro. All of the other ingredients are then
interesting background flavors, but the main flavor is the cilantro. If you make
a soup and call it a curry soup, it should taste like curry. Use enough so you
taste the curry in a balanced way, but not as an overwhelming flavor.

Another thing that I sometimes like to do is add solid ingredients into the bowl after the soup has been blended. The ingredients may be stirred into the soup, or left floating on top as a garnish. These solid ingredients may include: chopped avocado, chopped onions, zucchini spirals (made using the Saladacco machine or with a vegetable peeler), marinated or grated vegetables. Adding these types of ingredients to a soup can make it more hearty, satisfying, and interesting.

The soup recipes I will show you have been created using a Vita-Mix, which has a large container. If you only have a regular blender, you may have to divide the recipe in half, or blend the ingredients in multiple batches.

SOUP RECIPES

Thai Coconut Soup

2 cups **coconut** water
1 1/2 cups **water**
1 cup **tomatoes**
2 cups **young coconut meat**
1/2 **avocado**
1 medium **garlic clove**
1 inch **fresh ginger**
2 Tbsp. **mellow miso** (optional)
1 Tbsp. **garlic-flavored flax seed oil**, or olive oil
1/2 tsp. **sea salt**
2 Tbsp. **nama shoyu**, or tamari sauce
2 **limes** or **lemons**, juice of
2 pinches **cayenne pepper**, or to taste
1 cup **cilantro**, or parsley
1 cup **tomatoes**, diced
1/3 cup **onions**, chopped

Blend all ingredients except for the last three. Then add the cilantro or parsley, and blend briefly, so it is not entirely liquefied. Pour into a bowl. Add the last two ingredients and mix well. Add more cayenne pepper if you desire the soup to be spicier. Serves 4.

Kale-Coconut

1 cup **coconut water**
1 cup **young coconut meat**
2/3 cup **water**
2/3 cup **tomatoes**
1 cup **cucumbers**
1 cup **arugula**
1 cup **kale**
1 **apple**
2 **celery stalks**
1 **lime** or **lemon**, juice of
2 Tbsp. **mellow miso** (optional)
1 inch **fresh ginger**
1/3 cup **olive oil**
1 pinch **sea salt**

Blend all ingredients. Add more water if you need to. If young coconut is not available, you may use one avocado as a replacement.

Extra Zinc Soup

1 cup **cucumber**
1 **red bell pepper**
1 cup **arugula**
1 cup **parsley,** or cilantro
1/2 medium **avocado**
1/2 cup **pumpkin seeds**, ground
1/2 medium **apple**
1 cup **water**
3/4 tsp. **sea salt**
2 tsp. **nama shoyu**, or tamari sauce
2 Tbsp. **garlic-chili-flavored flax seed oil**, or olive oil
(if using olive oil, then add a pinch of cayenne pepper and 1 clove of fresh garlic)
spirulina flakes to taste (optional)

Blend all ingredients except spirulina flakes. Place in a bowl. If desired, add some spirulina flakes. Pumpkin seeds are one of the richest plant sources of zinc, so this is why we called this soup "Extra Zinc."

Cilantro Delight

1 cup **zucchini**
2 cups **cilantro**
1 medium **red bell pepper**
2 Tbsp. **nama shoyu**, or tamari sauce
1/2 tsp. **sea salt**
3 Tbsp. **almond butter**
1 **avocado**
1 1/2 cup **water**
spirulina flakes (optional)

Blend with water. Place in bowls. Sprinkle with spirulina flakes if desired.

Crème de Courgettes

1 cup **water**
1 Tbsp. **apple cider vinegar**
4 Tbsp. **olive oil**
1 Tbsp. **honey**, or 2 pitted dates
1 pinch **cayenne pepper**
1 tsp. **sea salt**
1 **lemon**, juice of
1 tsp. **cumin**
1 tsp. **dried oregano**
4 cups **zucchinis**, peeled
1/2 cup **cilantro**
6 Tbsp. **tahini**
1 Tbsp. **nama shoyu**, or tamari sauce (optional)

Blend. Pour into a bowl.

Add (as an optional garnish):
1 **zucchini**, grated or peeled into fine strips.
1 **yellow bell pepper**, chopped

Mix in the bowl with the soup. Serve.

Soupe du Jour

1 1/2 cups **tomato**
1 cup **cucumber**
1 small **red bell pepper**
1 stalk **celery**
1 cup **cilantro**
1 **lemon**, juice of
1 medium **garlic clove**
1 cup **clover sprouts**
1 **avocado**
1 tsp. **sea salt**
2 Tbsp. **nama shoyu**, or tamari sauce
2 cups **water**

Blend with distilled water until you reach a soupy consistency.
Place in a bowl.

Add: (don't blend)

4 Tbsp. **red onion**, chopped
1/2 **avocado**, cut into small cubes
1/2 cup **mango**, diced
1 pinch of **cayenne pepper** (optional)

Green Cream Soup

1 head **kale**
1/2 small head **cabbage**
1 **apple**
1/2 **jalapeño pepper**
1 large **avocado**
1 **lemon**, juice of
1 Tbsp. **nama shoyu**, or tamari sauce

Juice kale, cabbage, apple and jalapeño.
Pour into a blender or Vita-Mix. Blend
with the remaining ingredients.

I Live for Soups

1 cup **coconut water**
1 cup **zucchini**, or cucumber
1 cup **tomato**
1 **lemon**, juice of
1 small **avocado**
1/2 cup **parsley**
1/2 cup **cilantro**
1 tsp. **sea salt** (or, to taste)
2 Tbsp. **nama shoyu**, or tamari sauce
1 tsp. **jalapeño pepper**, or more to taste
2 Tbsp. **tahini**
4 Tbsp. **olive oil**
1/2 tsp. **Italian herb mix** (a mix of basil, thyme, oregano, and garlic)

Blend all ingredients together. If you own a Vita-Mix, you can double the quantities. If the soup is too thick, add some water.

Final touch:
    1 small **zucchini**, grated
    1/2 cup **tomato**, diced

Divide these non-blended vegetables into the soup bowls. Decorate with leaves of parsley.

Green Ginger

2 cups **tomato**, or cucumber, or a mix of both
1 cup **water**
4 cups **spinach**
1 medium **avocado**
1 inch **fresh ginger**
1 tsp. **sea salt**
1 tsp. **mellow miso**
1 **lemon**, juice of
2 Tbsp. **apple cider vinegar**
2 Tbsp. **olive oil**

Blend all ingredients. Serve.

Best Kale Soup

2 cups **water**
1 small **apple**
1 medium **tomato**
2 cups **kale**
1 cup **young coconut meat**, or 4 Tbsp. tahini
1/2 **avocado**
1 **garlic clove**
2 Tbsp. **flax seed oil**
2 Tbsp. **mellow miso**
2 Tbsp. **nama shoyu**, or tamari sauce
1 tsp. **sea salt**
1/2 **lime** or **lemon**, juice of
pinch **cayenne pepper** (to taste)

Blend the water, apple, tomato, and kale first. If using a regular blender, you will have to make half the recipe at a time. Add the remaining ingredients, except for cayenne pepper, then blend until smooth. Place in individual bowls. Sprinkle with a little cayenne pepper to taste.

Crème de Champignons

4 cups **mushrooms** (any kind)
2 cup soaked **cashews**, (or soft young coconut meat)
2 cups **water**
1 **tomato**
1 tsp. **sea salt**
2 Tbsp. **flax seed oil**
1 garlic **clove**
1 pinch **cayenne pepper**
2 Tbsp. **nama shoyu**, or tamari sauce
4 **green onions,** chopped

Blend all ingredients except for green onions. Place into bowls. Decorate with chopped onion.

Sunchoke Chowder

3 cups **sunchokes**, chopped (also called Jerusalem artichokes)
2 Tbsp. **flax seed oil**
1 pinch **cayenne pepper**, or 1 tsp. minced jalapeño pepper
1 medium **garlic clove** (optional)
2 cups of your **favorite greens**, such as parsley or kale
1 **lemon**, juice of
3 cups **water**
1 **avocado**
1 **apple**
2 Tbsp. **mellow miso**
2 Tbsp. **nama shoyu**, or tamari sauce
1/2 tsp. **sea salt**
paprika (to taste)

Blend all ingredients together in your Vita-Mix. If using a regular blender you will definitely need to make half the recipe at a time. Place into individual bowls. Sprinkle with cayenne pepper if desired.

Crème de Cèleri

3 cups ****celeriac**, peeled and diced
2 cups **water**
2 Tbsp. **mellow miso**
1/2 to 1 tsp. **sea salt**
2 Tbsp. **garlic-chile flavored flax seed oil**
    (if not available use flax seed oil or olive oil,
    and add 1 clove of garlic and a pinch of cayenne
    to the soup)
black pepper, to taste (optional)

Blend all ingredients, except for the black pepper. If you do not have a Vita-Mix, you may experience difficulty. You will have to make half of the recipe and dice the celeriac very small. Sprinkle with black pepper if desired. Serves 2.

** Celeriac is a weird-looking celery-related root that you can now find in many good health food and produce stores.

CHAPTER 16: GREEN DRINKS

Green drinks are made out of leafy greens such as kale, dandelion, chard, and spinach. They are strong drinks to be consumed both as a food and as medicine. Green drinks may be rendered more palatable by adding celery juice (also considered a green).

Green drinks made out of leafy greens are one of Nature's most powerful medicines. One green drink a day (or more) will increase your level of health dramatically. Green drinks will also help reduce your cravings for sugar and junk food.

Some naturopathic doctors prescribe large quantities of green drinks to people suffering from illnesses. Even if you are healthy to begin with, green drinks can work to boost and maintain your health.

The value of green drinks resides in their ability to make your body more alkaline. Most people, by eating foods that are acid-forming, such as meat, bread, pasta and most everything in the average diet, have an acid body condition (acidosis). Many vegetarians, and even raw-vegans, are also in this situation. Acid-forming foods in **The Sunfood Diet** include: nuts, seeds, some fruits, avocado, oils, and all fats. Pollution, anger, hate, and other negative emotions also trigger the tissues to produce more acids. We do need some acid-forming foods in our diet, but most of us consume so many acidic foods that we are not balanced.

HOW TO MAKE A GREEN DRINK

To make a good green drink, you need to use the right type of juicer. I have found that the Green Power and Green Life juicers are the best. You may also use a regular juicer, but the pulp may collect in it, and jam it. So invest in a Green Power or Green Life juicer, as they have been designed for green juices. If you are not able to invest in one at this point, you may consider investing in a less expensive manual or electric wheatgrass juicer. These juicers cost anywhere from $60 to $200, and are good for making green drinks.

WHAT TO JUICE?

All of the following vegetables can be juiced: celery, kale, spinach, chard, dandelion, parsley, collards, beet greens, and arugula; as well as any other leafy green vegetables. I rarely juice wheatgrass because I believe it to be an inferior green juice, made out of the hybrid seeds of wheat. I know there is a lot of hype around wheatgrass, but I have found that green drinks made out of wild or cultivated greens are much superior. Not that wheatgrass is never beneficial — because it is sometimes, especially when used properly in a detoxification program.

HOW MUCH TO DRINK?

I recommend starting with two to four ounces of green juice, mixed with six to ten ounces of celery juice. You may also add some cucumber and lemon juice. Increase the quantity of green juice, and decrease the quantity of celery juice up to the point where you are able to drink five to ten ounces of pure green juice straight. Drink this once or twice a day. If you need to get your body alkaline fast, drink four glasses (8 ounces each) of green juice a day.

David Wolfe, author of **The Sunfood Diet Success System***, believes that green juices are the most important addition we can make to our diet. Green juices are one of the keys to great health. So invest in a Green Power or Green Life juicer. Take the time to juice. It's worth it.*

GREEN JUICE RECIPES

The Athlete's Workout

1/2 medium **pineapple**, peeled and sliced
4 **apples**
6 **celery stalks**
1 bunch **parsley**

   Juice.

The New York City Survival Drink

8 **celery stalks**
1/2 bunch **arugula**
1 bunch **dandelion**
1 **lemon**, peeled

   Juice.

Antidote

1 head **kale**
8 **celery stalks**
1 **lemon**, peeled

   Juice. Drink as an "antidote" when you have gone overboard on acid-forming foods.

Winter Blues Killer

1 bunch **chard** (red or green)
1 small bunch **parsley**
4 **apples**

Juice.

Kale & Celery

5-6 **celery stalks**
3-4 large **kale leaves**
2-3 **chard leaves**, or bok choy

Juice everything. Then add the juice of half a lemon, and a pinch of cayenne pepper.

Booster drink

1 bunch **spinach**
1 bunch **parsley**
5-6 **celery stalks**
1 large **apple**

Juice everything. Then add the juice of one lime or lemon.

Jacumba Drink

2 **apples**
6 **kale leaves**

Juice everything. Because it uses ingredients available during the cold season, this drink constitutes a great winter food.

CHAPTER 17:
FRUIT JUICES & OTHER DRINKS

It is often nice to have fruit juice in the morning, or to enjoy one outside on a sunny day. Fruit juices, as they are high in sugar, are best appreciated in small to moderate quantities — or while doing a lot of exercise. Many people are in the habit of drinking lots of fruit juice all day, thinking that somehow they are improving their health that way. This is not a wise thing to do. Better to drink fruit juices in moderation, and focus more on green drinks to improve your health. Too much sugar, even when it is coming from natural fruit sources, is not good for you.

WHICH JUICER TO USE

To make great fruit juices you may use most juicers on the market. The Champion Juicer makes good fruit juices. The Green Power or Green Life juicers are designed for green juices, but can also work with fruit.

One of the best fruit juices for health is apple juice, because it is not too high in sugar, and contains many important nutrients. During the apple season, you may often find fresh "apple cider" for sale. Apple cider is nothing more than fresh pressed apple juice. Nowadays most apple cider is pasteurized, but it is still possible to find raw apple cider.

Apple juice is also satisfying and refreshing when mixed with celery juice. Jay Kordish "The Juiceman," who many Americans are familiar with from his TV infomercials, claims that he drinks apple-celery juice every day — and says it is his favorite drink.

I have provided a few fruit juice recipes, but they are only ideas. Fruit juice ideas are easy to come up with. Experiment and find your favorite combinations.

FRUIT JUICE RECIPES

Limonade d'été

5-6 **apples**
2 cups **grapes**
1/8 **lemon**

Juice everything, including the lemon and its peel. The peel of lemon contains bioflavanoids, which are powerful antioxidants.

Apple-Celery

5-6 **apples**
3-4 **celery stalks**

Juice. Good for hydrating the body on a hot summer day.

Apple-Strawberry

5-6 **apples**
1 cup **strawberries**

Juice the apples. Then pour the juice into a blender, add the strawberries, and blend.

Orange-Grapefruit

4 **oranges**
1 **grapefruit**
1 **lime**, or **lemon**

Peel fruit, then juice.

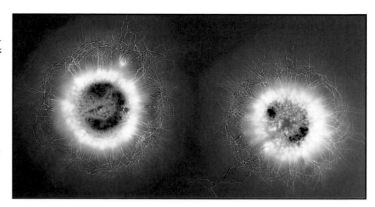

The Kirlian field of two oranges

Morning Drink

16 ounces **water**
1/2 **lemon**, or lime

Squeeze lemon or lime into the water. Drink first thing in the morning, everyday. Flushes the system, and helps you function better during the day.

Apple-Grape-Celery

5-6 **apples**
2 cups **grapes**
2 **celery stalks**

Juice. Good drink in the morning, as it contains many minerals (mainly from the celery), and natural sugar (from the fruit).

Green Watermelon

watermelon with the rind

Juice watermelon with the rind and seeds.

Cantaloupe & Honeydew

1 **cantaloupe**
1 **honeydew melon**

Juice cantaloupe and honeydew without seeds and rind (the rind of these melons are more bitter than that of watermelon).

Apple-Lemon

5-6 **apples**
1/2 **lemon**

Juice apples and squeeze the lemon half into the juice. Delicious.

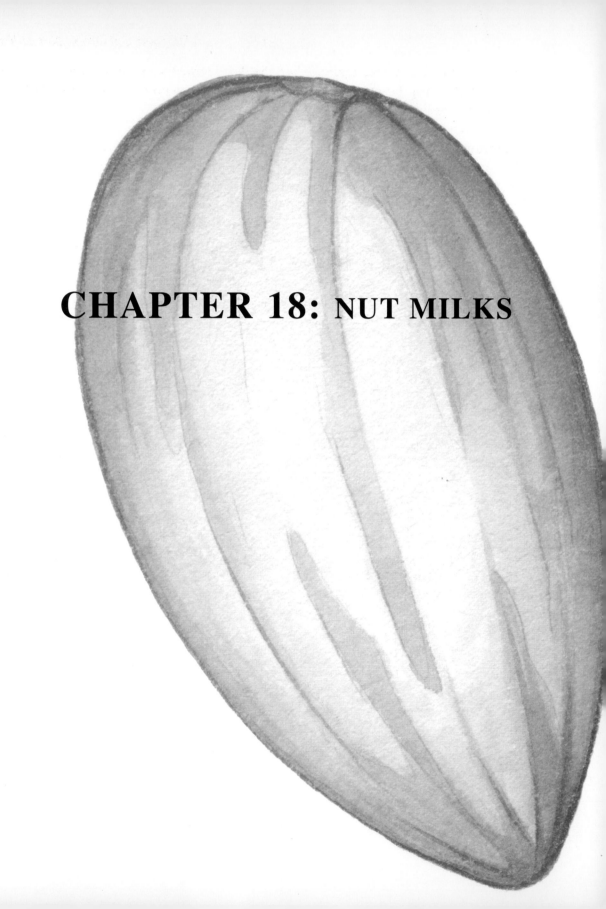

CHAPTER 18: NUT MILKS

Because of massive propaganda from the dairy industry, many people are in the habit of drinking large quantities of cow's milk everyday. Many believe that cow's milk is an essential part of good nutrition.

The truth is that most of what you have been told in school about milk is false. All of this information came from the dairy industry which was using all means possible to sell its products. You probably remember being told that milk builds strong bones. Is that true? Far from it. If this was true, then Americans and other milk-drinking nations would not have such a high incidence of osteoporosis, and other calcium-deficiency related conditions. Many nations, particularly in Asia, use almost no animal milk, and they have a low incidence of osteoporosis.

The idea that animal milk is essential for good nutrition of humans has no scientific basis. All mammals in Nature receive milk up to a certain age, after which they rely on their natural food for good nutrition. But humans seem to think that they should never be weaned, and have to rely on the milk of another animal for the rest of their lives. The truth is that the milk of cows is destined for only one type of creature: the calf.

If you are not already convinced that drinking animal milk is less than excellent, I recommend that you read the following books: **Don't Drink Your Milk**, by Dr. Frank A. Oski, M.D.; and **Diet for a New America**, by John Robbins.

Many people, after abandoning the habit of drinking animal milk, look for a replacement. Soymilk is a common milk substitute used in vegetarian circles. But soymilk is a processed food that has been sterilized at high temperatures. It does not contain much nutrition, and because it is cooked has no life-force.

The solution to this is raw nut milks. Nut milks are a great way to add highly digestible proteins to your diet. Nut milks are made out of soaked nuts or seeds, blended with water, and strained. When sweetened with dates, they are delicious additions to your menu. They may be enjoyed in the morning, or as a snack between meals. Nut milks are good for people who are sensitive to sugar, and will help you stay satisfied on your diet. They are rich in highly digestible proteins, fatty acids, and minerals.

To make a great nut milk, you must first soak the nuts and seeds that you are going to use. By soaking the nuts you will make them more digestible, as the enzymes lying dormant in the nuts become activated. You can soak the nuts for

8 to 12 hours. Dispose of the soaking water, and rinse the nuts before making the nut milk.

My friend, Laurie Cole, says that she uses ground flax seeds to thicken nut milk. She thinks that the flax seed meal slows down the absorption of the nut milk, and keeps you satisfied for a longer period of time. You may either buy the flax seeds, and grind them in a coffee grinder yourself, or you may buy the pre-made flax meal available at many health food stores.

The choice of your blender will also be a major factor in making a great nut milk. As discussed in chapter 12, the Vita-Mix is the best blender on the market, and will be of great help in making nut milks. You can also make the nut milk in a regular blender, but it will not be as smooth and digestible as those made using a Vita-Mix. You may also need to blend for a longer period of time, if you use a regular blender.

Nut milks need to be strained in order to remove particles from the nuts. For a rich creamy consistency, nut milks may be used in place of water in many soup recipes. You can also blend fruit into nut milks, or use nut milks as a base for smoothies. The following recipes will give you some ideas of what may be created with nut milks.

All nuts and seeds can be used for making nut milks, but I have found the best to be almonds, cashews, sunflower seeds, and sesame seeds.

Finally, nut milks may be safely kept in the refrigerator for a few days. But the water will tend to separate from the oil, so you will need to blend it again, or shake it vigorously before using. Nut milks may be made in large enough quantities two or three times a week, to provide a constant supply. But, be aware that they do have a lot of calories, so drink according to your needs.

BASIC METHOD FOR MAKING NUT MILKS

1. Soak one cup of either almonds, cashews, sunflower seeds, or sesame seeds overnight.
2. In the morning, dispose of the soaking water, and rinse the nuts or seeds.
3. Pour the nuts into your blender.
4. Add three to four times the quantity of water.
   (The less water you use, the thicker (creamier) your nut milk will be. Make sure that the water you use is of good quality — purified or distilled.)

5. Add one of the following: 2-4 Tbsp. honey or 6 pitted dates.
6. Blend at high speed.
    (If you use a Vita-Mix, you will need to blend only for 30 to 60 seconds.
    If you use a regular blender, you may have to blend for a few minutes.)
7. Pour the milk through a strainer into a container for refrigeration.

You may also;
• Add 2-4 Tbsp. of carob powder to turn it into chocolate milk.
• Blend with one frozen banana to turn it into a milk shake.
• Blend with other frozen fruits.
• Blend with fresh fruits.
• Combine everything previously mentioned.
• Experiment with whatever you fancy.

The recipe may be doubled or tripled, according to your needs.

NUT MILK RECIPES

Almond Milk

1 part **almonds**, soaked overnight
3-4 parts **water**
1 Tbsp. **honey**, or 2-3 pitted dates

Blend. Strain. Serve.

Banana Shake

2 cups **almond milk**
1 frozen **banana**
1-2 Tbsp. **honey**, or 2-5 pitted dates

Blend. Serve.

Chocolate Shake

2 cups **almond milk**
1 frozen **banana**
8 Tbsp. **carob powder**
2-4 Tbsp. **honey**, or or 5-10 pitted dates

Blend. Serve.

Orange Milk

1 part **almonds**, soaked overnight
3 parts **orange** juice

Blend. Strain. Serve.

Cashew Milk

1 cup soaked **cashews**
3 cups **water**
1 Tbsp. **honey**, or 2-3 pitted dates

Blend. There is almost no need to strain when using cashews, as they are so soft.

Berry Milk

2 cups **cashew milk**, or other nut milk
2/3 cup fresh or frozen **berries**
1- 2 Tbsp. **honey**, or 2-3 pitted dates

Blend all ingredients together.

Berry-Raisin Milk

2 cups **almond milk**, or cashew milk
1/2 cup fresh or frozen **berries**
1/2 cups **raisins**

Put the 1/2 cup of raisins into a bowl and cover with water. Let them soak
in water for 4-12 hours. Drain the water (you may drink raisin soak water,
or use it in place of water in smoothies), and pour one cup of soaked raisins
into the blender, along with the rest of the ingredients. Blend at high speed.

Cream Soda

1 cup soaked **almonds**
3 cups **water**
2-4 Tbsp. **honey**, or 5-10 pitted dates
1/2 tsp. **cardamom**

Blend and strain.

Cashew Cream

1 cup **cashews**
2 cups **water**
4 Tbsp. **honey**, or 8-10 pitted dates
1/2 tsp. pure **vanilla extract**

Blend at high speed and strain. This makes a thick cream that may be used
instead of dairy cream. If you still drink tea or coffee, you may use this
to replace cream or milk. You can also pour it into your fruit salads, or top
a sliced pear with the cream. It is also great with living pies, as well as
drizzled onto smoothies, fruit juices, and as a topping for raw ice cream.

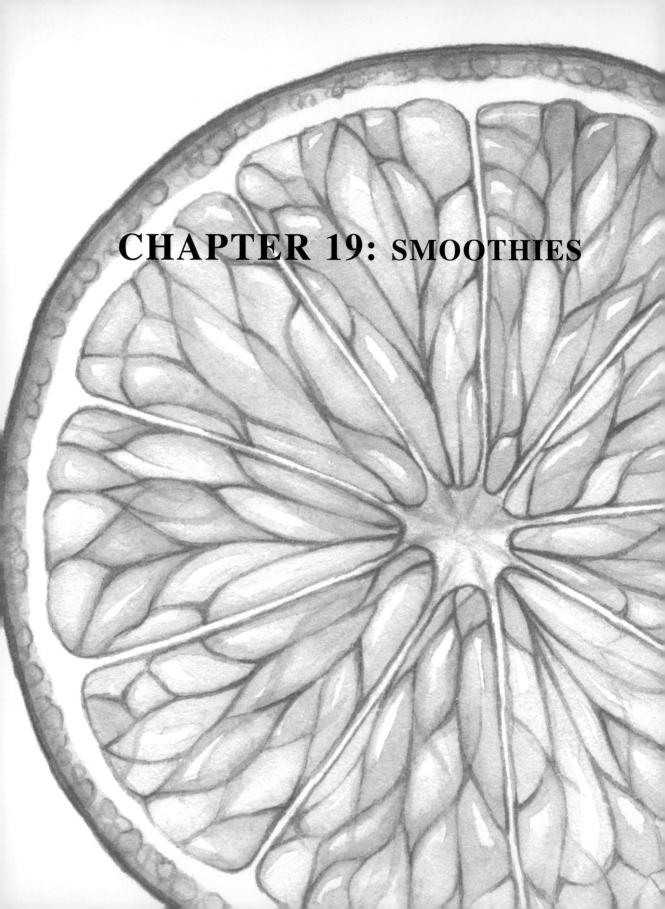

CHAPTER 19: SMOOTHIES

Smoothies are rich, thick, sweet, satisfying drinks made out of whole fruits, frozen fruits, fruit juices, and sometimes nuts, seeds, or other ingredients. Many people enjoy smoothies as a healthy meal. Smoothies are better and richer than fruit juices because they include the whole fruit, which both satisfies hunger and sweet cravings. If smoothies are made using nuts, seeds, or any type of fatty food, they will be absorbed slower, and help prevent the sugar rush some may experience with pure blended fruit.

Smoothies are made using a blender. You may also need a juicer to make the juice that you use for your smoothies, or use fresh store-bought juices. The best appliance is the Vita Mix, because it will make a better, smoother smoothie, in less time than a lower quality blender. Also, you will be able to make twice the amount using a Vita-Mix rather than a regular blender.

Fruit Juice — The most common juice bases for smoothies are apple juice and orange juice, but grape, pineapple, and other fruit juices also may be used.

Whole Fresh Fruits — Whole fresh fruits, such as apples, bananas, berries, peaches, mangos and papayas, may be used to make great smoothies. The fruit should be sliced first, in order to blend smoothly.

Frozen Fruits — Frozen fruits, such as bananas, berries and mangos, may be used to thicken smoothies. An advantage to using frozen fruits is that you get to use fruits that are not necessarily in season, such as berries or mangos. You can freeze the fruits yourself, or purchase packages of organic frozen fruits (especially berries) at your health food store.

Nuts and Seeds — Ground nuts and seeds (especially flax seeds), may be used in order to thicken a smoothie and make it heartier and more satisfying. They also add nutrition to a smoothie by providing high-quality proteins and essential fatty acids. The most common seeds to use are flax seeds. You will have to grind the flax seeds first in your coffee grinder, or use pre-made flax meal. If you blend whole flax seeds directly, they probably will not liquefy properly, and may not be fully digestible. Nuts may also be used. Soaked nuts may be put directly into the blender.

Oils — Cold pressed oils, such as hemp seed oil (wonderful in smoothies), and flax seed oil may be used in place of nuts and seeds. Also in this category is the avocado, which may be used to both thicken smoothies, and add wonderful flavor. Avocados are not only for guacamole and salads. Remember, avocados are a fruit.

Sweetener — Sweeteners may be used to make the smoothie more of a treat to satisfy a sweet tooth. Sweeteners that can be used include honey, dates, and dried fruits. Remember that all the fruit juices and whole fruits will make your smoothies quite sweet in the first place.

Flavorings — Flavorings may be added to your smoothies. Flavorings that may be used include pure vanilla extract, cinnamon, carob powder, cardamom and other spices.

Ice — Most juice bars put ice into their smoothies in order to save money on the overall cost of the ingredients. Ice is cheaper than frozen fruit. There are times though when ice may be useful in smoothies, such as when no frozen fruits are used. A hot summer day may also call for ice in a favorite smoothie.

Water — Add water if you need to or if you desire a lighter smoothie.

These are the basic ingredients used in the typical smoothie. Not all of them have to be present to make a great smoothie. Experiment and find what you enjoy the most. The smoothie recipes provided should give you some ideas.

SMOOTHIE RECIPES

Tropicanada

1/2 medium ripe **pineapple**
1 medium **mango**
2 **oranges**
water of 1 **young coconut**

Peel all the fruit, remove seeds, put in blender, blend at high speed.

Sweet Milk

1 **honeydew melon**, peeled and seeded
2 Tbsp. **honey**, or 2-3 pitted dates

Blend. Serve.

Green Dreams

1 small **cantaloupe**, flesh of
1 **peach**
2 **oranges**, juice of
1 **lime**, or half a lemon, juice of
1 tsp. **spirulina**
1 Tbsp. **honey**, or 2-3 pitted dates

Blend. Serve.

Papaya-Orange

2 cups **papaya**
1 1/2 cups **orange juice**
1 tsp. **hemp seed oil**

Blend. Serve.

Persimmon Madness

5 **persimmons**, without skin
2 cups **orange juice**
1 cup fresh or frozen **berries**

Blend. Serve.

Pear-Apple

1 **apple**
1 **pear**
1/2 cup **coconut water**
1 Tbsp. **honey**, or 2-3 pittted dates
2 Tbsp. ground **flax seeds**

Cut apple and pear into chunks, discarding the cores.
Blend with the rest of the ingredients.

Orange-Avo

3 to 4 **oranges**
3 to 4 **pitted dates**
1/2 **avocado**
1 **banana**

Blend. Serve.

Tangerine Dreams

1 cup **tangerine juice**
2 **bananas**
2 cups **papaya**

Blend. Serve.

Avocado

Iced

1 cup **tangerine juice**
1 Tbsp. **honey**, or 2-3 pitted dates
1 cup **ice**

In a blender, put juice first, then honey or dates, then ice. Blend.

Iced #2

1/2 cup **carrot juice**
1/2 cup **apple juice**
1 cup **ice**
1 Tbsp. **honey**, or 2-3 pitted dates

In a blender, put juice first, then honey or dates, then ice. Blend.

This drink rules!

Mango Dreams

2 cups **orange juice**
2 cups **mango flesh** (about 3 to 4 mangoes)

Blend for creamy heaven.
Optional: Blend with 1 tsp. of spirulina for a fortified green drink.

June Smoothie

2 cups **papaya**
20-30 **pitted cherries**

Blend. Serve.

Magic Potion

1 cup **orange juice**
2 **mangos**, flesh of
8 ozs. (small package) fresh or frozen **blueberries**
1 frozen, or fresh, **banana**
2 Tbsp. ground **flax seeds**
1 Tbsp. **honey**, or 1-2 pitted dates

Blend. Serve.

Green Mango

1 cup **orange juice**
2 **mangos**, flesh of
1 **avocado**

Blend. Serve.

Super-Smoothie

1 cup **orange juice**
1 big **apple**, peeled and seeded
1 cup **strawberries**
1 Tbsp. **ground flax seeds**
1 Tbsp. **honey**, or 2-3 pitted dates

Blend. Serve.

Watermelon Surprise

4 cups **watermelon**, with seeds
4 Tbsp. **ground flax seeds**

Blend.

Nectarine

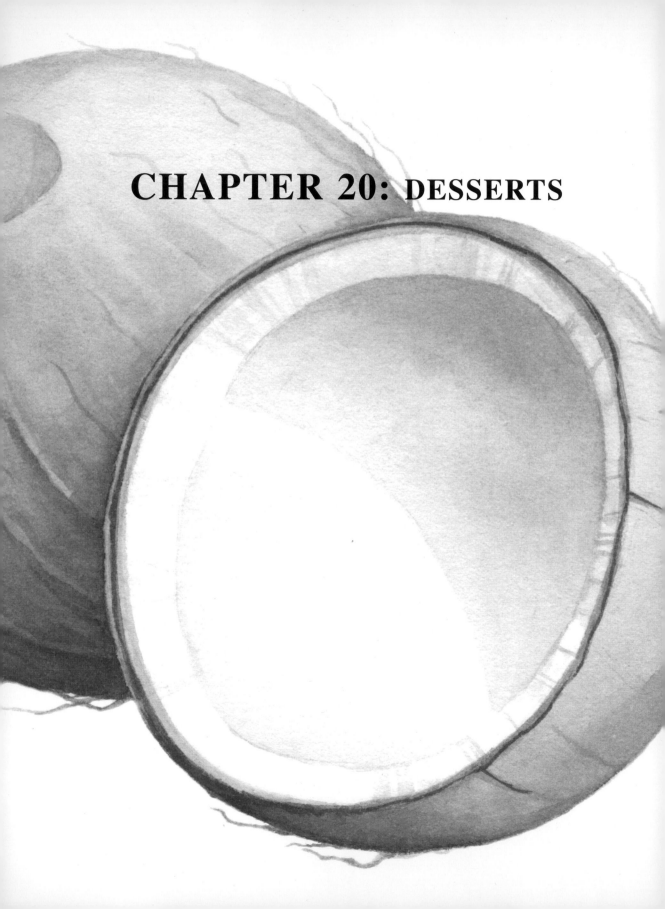

CHAPTER 20: DESSERTS

Who does not enjoy pie, ice cream, chocolate and other sweet treats? Most of us are huge fans of dessert! For many, enjoying dessert is a guilty pleasure to be indulged in on a regular basis. We know dessert is not the best thing for us, but we cannot resist the temptation. Even though the price we pay may be extra pounds, most choose to pay it, because the pleasure of eating dessert is so great! Greater than the pain of putting on extra weight!

So does changing to a diet based on raw fruits and vegetables mean that you have to give up desserts, even on special occasions? Hardly! Be relieved that it is possible to create a variety of treats using natural foods. Not only will they satisfy your desire for dessert, but they will be healthy for you too!

Using combinations of nuts, fresh and dried fruits, honey, carob, and other ingredients, you can create a variety of sweet things, from pies to ice cream, without having to use refined sugar or flour. These raw treats will probably amaze you. I know some of you have a hard time believing that something made out of nuts and fruits could be more delicious than a chocolate cake, but you will just have to try it for yourself...

The **Sunfood Diet** desserts are artistic creations, made using the following ingredients:

Fruits — Many people, rather than finishing their meals with a slice of pie or a scoop of ice cream, have fruit for dessert. Fresh fruits are often the basis of **Sunfood Diet** desserts. Any fruits you like are appropriate, such as mangos, papayas, apples, bananas, peaches, and pineapples. Fruits can be sliced, blended, and added to pies, shakes, or simply incorporated into fruit salads.

Dried Fruits — Dried fruits (especially dates) are often used to sweeten raw desserts, and help create a nice texture. They are particularly delicious when incorporated with nuts. In fact, nuts and dried fruits eaten together are a great simple dessert. Dried fruits and dates may be soaked, blended into sweet concoctions, used in raw pie crusts, or used in other creations.

Nuts and Seeds — Nuts are the "flour" of the **Sunfood Diet** desserts. They provide creaminess and richness, as well as flavor and nutrition. They may be turned into piecrusts, blended into shakes, or mixed in other ways with dried fruits for a stunning result. The best and most flavorful nuts to use include: almonds, coconuts, cashews, Brazil nuts, walnuts, pecans, hazelnuts, and pine nuts. Seeds, such as sesame seeds, and nut butters may also be used in the creation of raw desserts.

Other Sweeteners — Besides dried fruit, honey may also be used to sweeten raw desserts.

Carob Powder — Carob powder, which can be obtained in all health food stores, is a delicious replacement for chocolate, whenever a chocolate flavor is desired.

Flavorings — Vanilla, cinnamon, and other flavorings may be used to make your raw desserts sparkle.

Within **The Sunfood Cuisine** recipes, these ingredients will be mixed in an original way to create amazing desserts! You will find though, that no matter what you do, combining any of these ingredients will achieve great results. First, try some of the dessert recipes as outlined. This should give you many ideas on how to start making your own creations. Remember, all it takes is a little imagination… and lots of good ingredients!

An electromagnetic Kirlian photo of an avocado cut in half
(photo by Christopher Wodtke, www.kirlian.com)

DESSERT RECIPES

Coconut Cream

1 cup soaked **pine nuts**
1 cup fresh, ****shredded coconut**
2 Tbsp. **honey**, or 2-3 dates
6 soaked **apricots**

> Blend all ingredients in a food processor or heavy-duty blender. Serve as a dip with fruits, or on top of a raw pie. You can also purchase unsweetened shredded coconut that is available in most health food stores.

> ***To make shredded coconut, buy the "mature" coconuts (the brown ones sold in most markets), crack them open, remove the hard white meat, and shred in a food processor, a Champion juicer, or by hand with a grater.*

Ice Cream

frozen, peeled **bananas**
frozen fruits (mangos, berries, etc.)

> Process the frozen bananas using your Champion or Green Power juicer with the blank plate on. There is simply no other alternative — you must do it that way to reach that insane ice cream consistency. Then process smaller amounts of other frozen fruits as a flavoring. The base remains frozen bananas. You may also add fresh fruits, nut butters, cinnamon, or carob.

Avocado Ice-Cream

1 medium **avocado**
5-6 **dates**
3-4 frozen **bananas**

> Using your Champion or Green Power juicer with the blank plate on, process dates first with the avocado, then the bananas. Mix well.

> *Note: Do not take time to clean the juicer, eat immediately!*

Vanilla Ice Cream

1 cup pitted **dates**
1 cup **pine nuts**, not soaked
1 cup **water**
1/2 tsp. **pure vanilla extract**

Blend all ingredients together in a food processor or heavy duty blender. Pour into a bowl and freeze for at least two hours.

Carob Treat

2 cups **avocado**, mashed
2 cups **dates**
1/2 cup **carob powder**
water, as needed for consistency

Blend all ingredients in a food processor or heavy-duty blender. You may also use a food processor. Add the avocado first, then the dates, then the remaining ingredients. Use water, if needed, to reach desired consistency.

Real Chocolate

2 cups **avocado**, mashed
2 cups **dates**
4 Tbsp. **organic cocoa powder**
water, or nut milk

Try this vegan chocolate recipe the next time you have a chocolate craving, if you don't object to cocoa powder.

Vanilla Custard

2 cups young **coconut flesh**
1 cup pitted **dates**
1/3 cup **coconut water**
1/2 tsp. **pure vanilla extract**

Blend all ingredients together until totally smooth. You may use a food processor for this. The custard can be eaten plain, or with fresh fruits. Serve as a cream poured over a bowl of berries for a great treat. Serve in individual bowls with a mint leaf for garnish. Better than any commercial vanilla pudding out there!

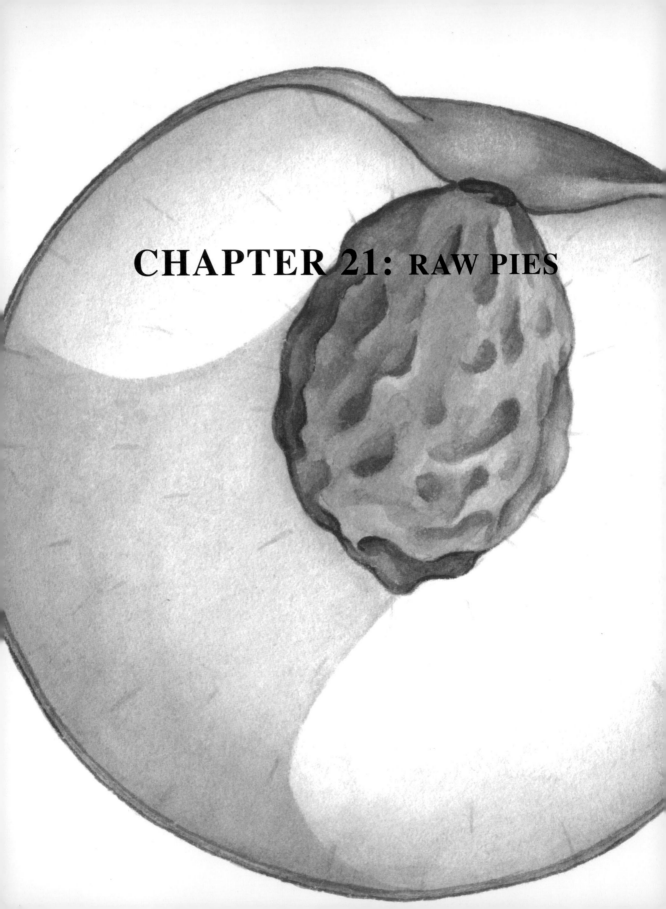

CHAPTER 21: RAW PIES

Who said that pies have to be cooked? The best pies I have ever tasted were raw pies! Raw pies are so rich in flavor, they are sure to surprise you. These raw pies are simply bursting with incredible flavor because all of the vitality contained in the fruits and nuts is still intact.

The idea behind a raw pie is simple. First, you will have to use a typical pie container, ideally a glass one. Second, you will make a crust out of nuts and dates, and fill it with a fruit mixture. Often we will top the pie with a sweet topping made out of nuts and either dates or honey.

THE CRUST

To make the crust, I usually use soaked nuts and dates, or other dried fruits, and blend these in a food processor. It is quite difficult to make the crust any other way, because the food processor is the only tool that really creates the crust consistency that I want with the nuts. The crust "dough" is pressed into a glass pie container, which is put in the freezer for an hour or two.

BASIC CRUST RECIPE

2 cups **walnuts**
1 cup soaked **almonds**
10-15 **dates**
2 Tbsp. **orange juice**

Put the nuts in the food processor with the dates. Blend them while adding the orange juice. You should end up with a big ball of sticky nut mixture. If you run the nuts through a Champion juicer, you will obtain a nut butter consistency, which is not what we want. If you do not have a food processor, you may also grind the nuts in a Vita-Mix, a little at a time, and place the mixture in a bowl to be mixed with the dates by hand.

Once you have obtained your crust "dough," you will press it inside, and all around, the pie container with your wet fingers. Make it look like a normal pie crust. You may need to repeatedly dip your fingers in water to prevent the dough from sticking to your fingers as you spread it. Then I usually place the pie container in the freezer while I prepare the rest of the pie.

PIE FILLINGS

Pie fillings may be made out of anything sweet. You can fill the crust with sliced bananas topped with sliced fruit, and top it with a sweet topping. Or you can blend fruits, such as papayas and mangos, along with some nuts to thicken the mixture, and pour this mixture inside the pie before freezing for an hour. You can also make a thick, sweet pie filling out of dates and nuts such as pecans, and flavor this with cinnamon or cloves. Then pour the sweet mixture into the pie crust, and decorate with pine nuts, macadamia nuts, shredded coconut, slices of fruit, or berries. You could also create a combination of everything I mentioned, and make a layered pie. Just be creative, and get inspired by the pie recipes that I provide. For an amazing taste, add a creamy, sweet topping to your pie. You can also top your pie with sliced fruit or whole berries. Leaves of mint can also be used to decorate a pie.

Apple

PIE RECIPES

Divine Mango Pie

Crust:
See basic crust recipe, as described on **page 177.**

First Layer:
2 cups pitted, **soft dates**
2 Tbsp. **pine nuts**
2 Tbsp. **sliced almonds**
2 Tbsp. **orange juice**

> If you do not have soft dates, you will need to soak your dates in water for one hour. Pit all the dates, mix all ingredients together, then spread on top of the piecrust.

*Second Layer***:**
3 **mangos**, peeled and sliced
6 **ripe apricots**, pitted and chopped
10 **strawberries**, sliced very thin

> Mix all ingredients together, then spread over the date mixture.

Topping:
2 cups **macadamia nuts**
1 cup **coconut water**
4 Tbsp. **honey** or 8-10 dates (optional)
1 tsp. **vanilla**

> Blend all ingredients together, then pour on top of the pie.

> For a final touch, sprinkle with pine nuts, raisins, and add slices of strawberries in the center.

Yam Pie

Crust:
See basic crust recipe, as described on **page 177.**

Yam Filling:
4 **yams** (medium to small), peeled
1 medium **avocado**
1 cup **dates**
3 Tbsp. **honey** or 6-8 dates (optional)
1 tsp. **vanilla**
1 tsp. **cinnamon**

> Cut the yams into pieces small enough to fit into a Champion juicer. Run the yams, avocado, and dates through your Champion or Green Power juicer with the blank plate on. Add the rest of the ingredients. Pour evenly into the crust. Top with fresh shredded coconut, and slices of strawberries.

Tarte aux Fruits

Crust:
See basic crust recipe, as described on **page 177.**

First layer:
2 cups soaked **raisins** (soaked for at least one hour)
1 cup **soft dates** (soak for 1 hour if hard)
1/2 **avocado**, mashed
2 Tbsp. **almond butter**
1 **lemon,** juice of
a little **water**, from the soaking of the raisins
2 Tbsp. **carob powder**

> Mix in a bowl (don't blend), and pour into pie crust.

Second layer:
2 cups of diced fruits, or slices of juicy fruits (choose one or more of the following, depending on what is in season: papayas, mangos, cherimoyas, apricots, cherries, raspberries, blueberries, peaches, bananas, or pears)

> Spread over the raisin-date mixture. Top with fresh, shredded coconut.

Apple Pie

Crust:
See basic crust recipe, as described on **page 177.**

Filling:
3 cups shredded **apples**
1 cup soaked **raisins**
1 1/2 cup soaked **cashews**
1/4 tsp. **nutmeg**
1/2 tsp. **cinnamon**
1/2 cup **raisin soak water**
2 Tbsp. **honey** or 3-4 dates (optional)

Shred apples using a hand-shredder, or a food processor. Place the 3 cups shredded apples in a bowl. Mix in the raisins. The raisins have to be soaked in advance. I recommend soaking one cup. Cover them with water in a bowl. They will almost double in size when soaked, but you can use the extra for other purposes (adding to salads, eating as snacks, in other dessert recipes, etc.). In the blender, make a sauce out of the cashews, nutmeg, cinnamon, raisin soak water, and honey. Raisin soak water is the water in which the raisins have been soaking. The longer the raisins have been soaking, the sweeter the water will be. Mix this sauce with the shredded apples and raisins. Pour the mixture into the pie crust. Decorate with slices of fruits (bananas, apples, strawberries, etc.).

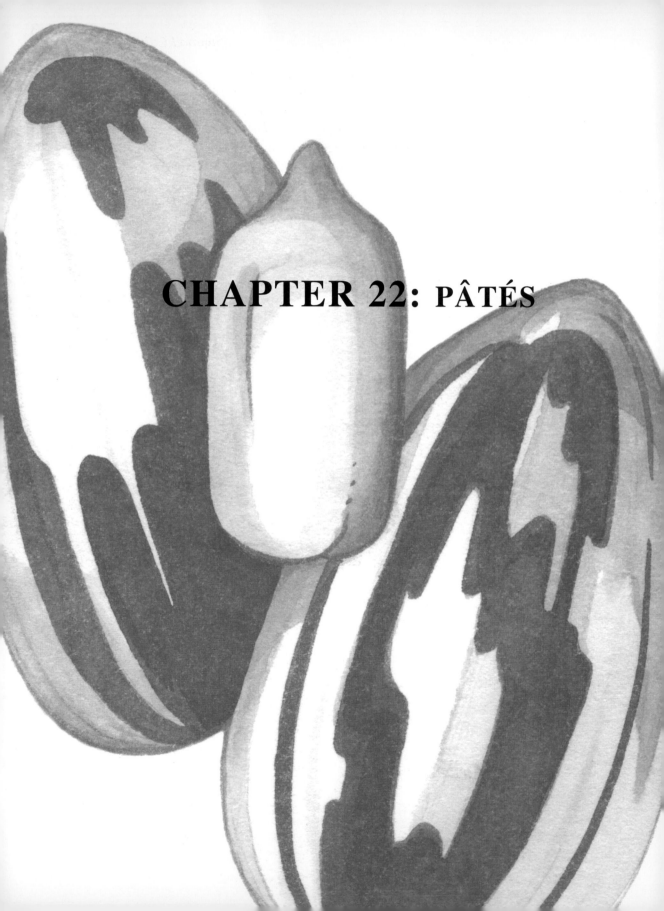

CHAPTER 22: PÂTÉS

Raw vegan pâtés are rich savory spreads made out of nuts, seeds, and sometimes vegetables. Nut pâtés are rich in protein and fat, and usually eaten as a side dish along with green vegetables, or spread onto carrots, celery, and raw crackers. Green vegetables will help with the digestion of the pâtés since nuts and seeds are acid forming, and greens are alkaline forming. Nut pâtés may be useful for people who are looking for some heavier food to replace the cheeses they were used to eating. But nut pâtés are concentrated foods containing lots of fat, so you should be careful to not overeat them.

To make a nut pâté, I first soak the nuts and seeds. It makes them easier to digest, and also easier to blend. I suggest that you soak the nuts overnight in purified or distilled water. I use a Champion or Green Life juicer, with the blank plate on, to puree the nuts. If you do not have one of these juicers, you can also use a food processor, but you will not achieve the same consistency. You can also mix some vegetable puree (such as carrot, broccoli, or cauliflower, that has been pureed using a food processor or Champion/Green Power juicer) with the nuts. Depending on how rich you want your pâté to be, you may vary the quantity of vegetables used.

After I have pureed the nuts and seeds, I usually add some chopped herbs, vegetables (such as tomatoes or peppers), seasonings (which usually comprise something salty), and a spice such as curry or turmeric. The pulp left over from juicing vegetables works great in pâtés. I also often like to add a little extra cold-pressed oil, to make the pâté more rich and flavorful. Lemon juice or apple cider vinegar may also be added to enhance the flavor, and give it a "bite."

CATEGORIES OF FOOD IN A NUT PÂTÉ

Soaked Nuts and Seeds — The nuts and seeds are pureed to achieve a rich, creamy consistency.

Vegetables (optional) — If desired, some hard vegetables, such as carrot and broccoli, can be pureed using a juicer, or a food processor. The fewer vegetables you use, the more rich your pâté will be.

Chopped Vegetables and Herbs — After the pâté has been made, chopped herbs (dill, basil, etc.) soft vegetables, and non-sweet fruits (tomato, pepper, etc.) may be added.

Salty Seasoning — A nut pâté should have some sort of salty seasoning in it. Seasonings that may be used include sea salt, nama shoyu (or tamari sauce), dulse flakes, kelp, and miso. Chopped olives may also be added.

Spices — A spice of your choice can be added. Favorite spices for pâtés include cumin, curry powder, and turmeric. This category also includes minced garlic and ginger, which may be added to the nut pâté. Lemon juice or apple cider vinegar can also be added to enhance the flavor of the pâté.

Cold-Pressed oil (optional) — To create a pâté with a very rich flavor, we may use a little bit of cold-pressed oil, such as olive oil or flax seed oil. However, you should remember that there is already a lot of oil in the nuts, so use additional oil in moderation.

BASIC NUT PATÉ RECIPE

2 cups soaked **nuts and seeds** of your choice. (My favorites include: sunflower seeds, almonds, sesame seeds, and pumpkin seeds)

2 cups pureed **hard vegetables** of your choice (carrots, beets, cauliflower, broccoli, etc.)

1/2 cup chopped **fresh herbs** of your choice (cilantro, parsley, or dill, etc.).

1/2 cup diced **tomato** or red bell pepper (optional).

2 Tbsp. **nama shoyu** or tamari sauce, 1 tsp. of sea salt, dulse flakes or kelp to taste, miso to taste, or a mix of all of these.

The saltiness of the nut pâté depends on your preference.

1 tsp. **spice** of your choice, such as curry, cumin, and turmeric.

2 Tbsp. **lemon juice** or apple cider vinegar (optional).

2 Tbsp. **cold-pressed oil** of your choice, such as flax seed oil or olive oil.

Process all the nuts in your Champion or Green Power juicer with the blank plate on, or use a food processor. Alternate with the vegetables. Place the mixture into a bowl. Add all the other ingredients, then mix well. Serve with plenty of green vegetables cut for dipping. You may also spread the pâté into celery sticks, then cut them into two or three-inch servings.

Feel free to experiment away from the guidelines, and try your own variations. Remember that recipes are only ideas! Follow them one time, then experiment with your own variations.

Bell Pepper

Super-Pâté

2 cups soaked **sunflower seeds**
1/4 cup **black sun-dried olives** pitted, chopped
2 Tbsp. **olive oil**
1 Tbsp. **lemon juice**
2 Tbsp. **nama shoyu**, or tamari sauce
1/2 Tbsp. **turmeric**

> Process the sunflower seeds in a Champion or Green Power juicer with the blank plate on. Place into bowl. Mix in all other ingredients. Serve with green vegetables.

Wild Rice Pâté

2 cups **sunflower seeds**
1 cup sprouted **wild rice ****
2 Tbsp. **flax seed oil**
1 tsp. **curry powder**
1/2 cup chopped, **sun-dried olives**
sea salt (optional)

> Process the sunflower seeds and the wild rice in a Champion or Green Power juicer to create a pâté. Place in a bowl. Mix in all the other ingredients. Serve with flax seed crackers **(page 209)** and fresh vegetables.
> ** For instructions on sprouting wild rice, see **page 102.**

Almond-Carrot Pâté

2 cups soaked **almonds**
2-3 large **carrots**

> Process through a Champion or Green Power juicer with the blank on. Alternate between carrots and almonds. You may also use a food processor, but would likely achieve a less desirable result.

Add to the mixture:
1 **tomato**, chopped
water (as needed)
2 **lemons,** juice of
4-6 **green onions**, chopped
1 handful of **whole dulse**, or dulse flakes

> Serve as a base for <u>Nori Rolls,</u> or in bell peppers cut in half, or as a raw sandwich inside leaves of romaine lettuce.*Tip: If you add too many carrots, the pâté may be too juicy. Try to find the optimal balance to achieve a real pâté consistency.*

Pâté de Chez-Nous

1 cup **almonds**, soaked overnight
1 cup **sunflower seeds**, soaked 6-8 hours
1 **red bell pepper**, diced
1-2 Tbsp. **nama shoyu** or tamari sauce, or 1/2 tsp. sea salt (optional)
10-20 **olives**, chopped
1 tsp. **kelp**
1/2 cup of **fresh herbs** (basil, cilantro, or Italian parsley)
2 Tbsp. **lemon juice**

Using a food processor or Champion/Green Power juicer using the blank plate, process the almonds and sunflower seeds. Add red bell pepper, nama shoyu, or tamari sauce, olives, herbs, lemon juice, and kelp. Mix well.

Pâté d'Italie

1 cup **sunflower seeds**
1 cup **pumpkin seeds**

Soak all the seeds overnight in pure water. Process through a food processor, or Champion/Green Power juicer, or blender.

Add:
1/2 cup **basil**, chopped
1/2 **red onion**, chopped
2 Tbsp. **nama shoyu**, or tamari sauce

Mix all ingredients together.

An electromagnetic Kirlian photo of broccoli
(photo by Christopher Wodtke, www.kirlian.com)

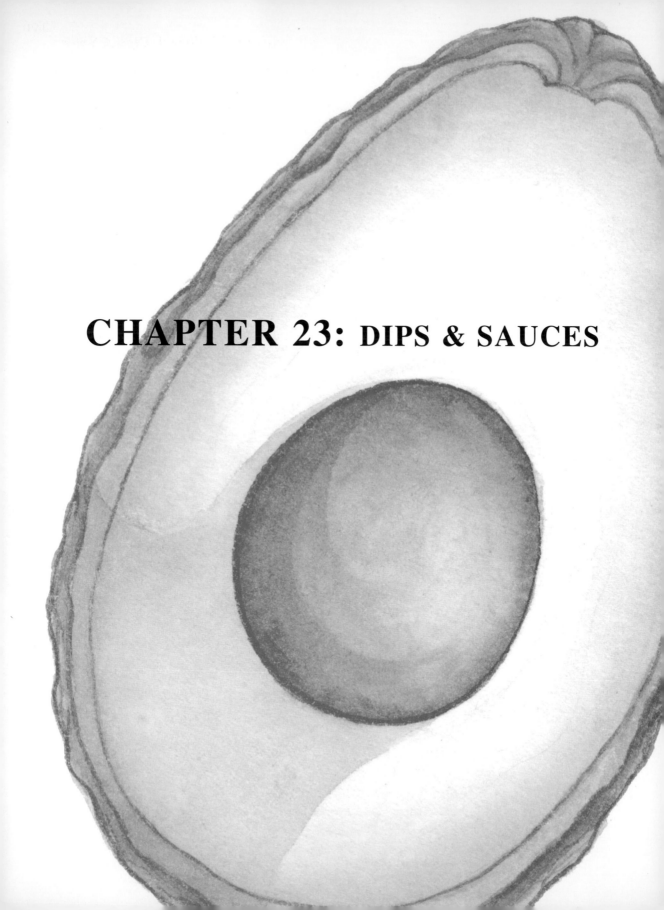

CHAPTER 23: DIPS & SAUCES

Everyone is familiar with guacamole, salsa, and other dips. These dips are made from fruits and vegetables. They are often served as an entrée with vegetables or as a side dish. In **The Sunfood Cuisine**, things are slightly different. Guacamole can be viewed as a staple. In addition, dips and sauces may form the basis of a meal.

Some of these dips are so delicious that you will want to eat them as a meal, with plenty of green vegetables. You can also prepare extra for use on other salads and snacks.

Dips and sauces are not as rich as nut pâtés, since they are made with avocados, tomatoes and oils, rather than nuts and seeds. I usually make dips in a food processor or a blender. However, in the case of making guacamole, all you need is a bowl, a cutting board, a spoon, fork, and knife.

Ingredients used consist of the following:

Avocado
The basic ingredient of guacamole, avocados, can be used as an ingredient in many sauces and dips. The creaminess and richness of the avocado is perfect for these.

Oil, Miso, Nuts and Seeds
Cold pressed oil, miso, and nuts may be used in dips. Tahini, which is sesame butter, is also often used.

Tomatoes and Vegetables
We often like to add diced tomatoes to many dips, especially guacamole. Other vegetables may be blended with avocado, oils, or nuts to make a great vegetable dip.

Herbs and Spices
Fresh herbs, dried herbs, and spices may be used in dips to enhance flavor.

Salty Seasonings
Salty seasonings are essential in many dips. Our choices include: sea salt, nama shoyu (or tamari sauce), miso, and dulse flakes.

Lemon Juice
Lemon juice, or lime juice, as well as apple cider vinegar, may be used in dips and sauces to provide a tangy bite.

There is no basic recipe for dips. The idea is to make something creamy enough to use as a dip that will cling to dipped vegetables. We use: avocado, nuts, seeds, and oil to make dips creamy. Flavorings include: herbs, spices, sea salt, and lemon juice. We often add vegetables, such as diced tomatoes, peppers, onions, or minced garlic. Get inspired by the following recipes, and eventually come up with your own favorite dips and sauces!

DIPS & SAUCES RECIPES

Super Guac

2 cups **avocados**, mashed
1 1/2 cup **tomatoes**, diced
1/2 **yellow bell pepper,** chopped
1/2 cup **cilantro**, chopped
1 **lemon,** juice of
2 Tbsp. **tahini**
4 Tbsp. **flax seed oil**
1/4 to 1/2 tsp. **sea salt** (to taste)
1 tsp. **cumin**
1 tsp. **garlic powder**
cayenne pepper (to taste)

> Mash the avocados in a bowl. Add all of the other ingredients. Mix well. Serve with vegetables, or inside leaves of romaine lettuce or cabbage for a raw burrito.

Arugula Guac

2 medium **avocados**, mashed
1 cup **tomatoes**, diced
1 1/2 cups **arugula**, chopped
1 **lime, juice of**
1 Tbsp. **apple cider vinegar**
2 Tbsp. **flax seed oil**
1/4 to 1/2 tsp. **sea salt** (to taste)

> Mash the avocados in a bowl. Add all of the other ingredients. Mix well.

Peamoli

2 cups fresh or frozen **green peas**
2 Tbsp. **olive oil**
1 **lemon,** juice of
1 medium **garlic clove**
1/4 to 1/2 tsp. **sea salt** (to taste)
1 tsp. **dulse powder** (optional)
1/2 cup **tomatoes**, diced (cherry tomatoe halves are best)

Blend all ingredients, except the tomatoes, in your Vita-Mix or food processor. You may also homogenize the peas in a Champion or Green Life juicer with the blank plate on, and add the other ingredients separately in a bowl. Add diced tomatoes, then mix well. If you use frozen peas (organic only), you will have to let them thaw overnight. Add the dulse powder if you prefer a "smoky" flavor. Serve with sticks of celery, carrots, peppers, and green vegetables.

Cream Cheese

1 cup **avocado**, mashed
4 Tbsp. **tahini**
2 Tbsp. **orange juice**
1/4 to 1/2 tsp. **sea salt**
1 Tbsp. **nama shoyu**, or tamari sauce
1 tsp. **Italian herb mix** (a mix of basil, thyme, oregano, and garlic), or herbs of your choice (dill, basil, cilantro, etc)

Blend all ingredients together in a food processor. Alternatively, simply mix in a bowl. Serve with green vegetables.

Mediterranean Guacamole

2 cups **avocado**, mashed
1 cup **tomato**, diced
1 big **lemon** (or two limes), juice of
1 medium **garlic clove**, minced
3 Tbsp. **fresh basil**, chopped
1 tsp. **Italian herb mix** (a mix of basil, thyme, oregano, and garlic)
2 Tbsp. **onion**, chopped
1 tsp. **kelp powder**
1/4 to 1/2 tsp. **sea salt** (to taste)
2 Tbsp. **olive oil**
1 pinch of **cayenne pepper**

Mash avocados in a bowl. Add all the other ingredients. Serve inside cabbage leaves, or use as a dip with green vegetables, root vegetables, or on top of flax seed crackers.

Mango Salsa

3 cups **tomato**, diced
2 cups fresh **mango**, diced
8 Tbsp. **onion**, minced
1/2 cup **cilantro**, chopped
2 **limes,** juice of
1 **garlic clove**, minced
2 tsp. **jalapeño pepper**, minced
1/4 tsp. **sea salt** (or to taste)

Mix all ingredients in a bowl.

Pineapple Chutney

2 cups **pineapple**, diced
1/2 small **red bell pepper**, diced
2 inches **fresh ginger**, grated
2 Tbsp. **apple cider vinegar**
1 Tbsp. **honey**
1/4 tsp. **sea salt**

Mix all ingredients in a bowl. Serve as a side dish with salad and vegetables, or on top of guacamole.

Spinach Dip

4 cups **spinach**, chopped
1/2 to 1 cup **water**
2 Tbsp. **apple cider vinegar**, or lemon juice
1/8 tsp. **nutmeg**
1/4 tsp. **sea salt**
2 small to medium **avocados**
1 cup **cucumber**

Blend all ingredients together in the Vita-Mix or food processor. Try to achieve a creamy, dip-like consistency. Use as little water as possible. This dip is refreshing, light, and good to serve with vegetables.

Avocado Mayonnaise

1 1/2 cups **avocados**, mashed
1/3 cup **olive oil**
1 Tbsp. **honey**, or 2-3 dates
1 **garlic clove**
6 Tbsp. **apple cider vinegar**
2 Tbsp. **orange juice**
2 Tbsp. **dulse flakes**
1/4 tsp. **sea salt**

Mix all ingredients in a food processor or blender, adjusting quantities to obtain a rich, mayo-like consistency.

Almond Mayonnaise

2 cups soaked **almonds**
2/3 cup **olive oil**
1/4 cup **apple cider vinegar**
2 tsp. **dill seeds,** or parsley flakes, or 1/2 cup of fresh dill
1 1/2 cups **tomato**
1/2 tsp. **sea salt**

Put almonds in a food processor or Vita-Mix, along with the apple cider vinegar, and tomato. Then pour in the olive oil a little bit at a time until you reach a creamy consistency. Add parsley flakes and sea salt. The Vita-Mix is the best tool for this recipe. The goal is to achieve a super-creamy consistency. If you are unable to do so, it may be because your food processor is not strong enough. You may also run the almonds through a Champion Juicer first, before blending all of the other ingredients together.

Olive Cream

15 **sun-dried olives**, pitted
2 cups **tomato**, or cucumbers (or 1 cup of each)
1 large **avocado**, or two small ones
2 Tbsp. **apple cider vinegar**, or lemon juice
1/4 tsp. **sea salt**

Blend all ingredients. A food processor can work for this. If you have some trouble making it blend, add a little water.

Super Dulse

2 oz. of **dulse**, rinsed briefly, then chopped
6 Tbsp. **tahini**
2 Tbsp. **apple cider vinegar**
1 **lemon,** juice of
1 tsp. **curry powder** (optional)
2 Tbsp. **olive oil**
1 cup **cucumber** (or tomatoes), chopped
1 cup **arugula**, chopped

Mix all ingredients in a bowl. Serve with vegetables or eat with a spoon.

Pico De Gallo

4 cups **tomato**, chopped
2 **limes**, diced
1/4 cup **onion**, diced
1 cup **pineapple**, diced
1 cup **cilantro**, chopped
2 Tbsp. **apple cider vinegar**
1 tsp. **cumin**
1 tsp. **sea salt**
cayenne pepper or minced chiles to taste

The tomatoes, onions, and pineapple should be diced finely. Mix. Add enough cayenne pepper powder or minced chiles (hot peppers) to make this salsa spicy, without being overly hot. Serve on top of Flax Crackers **(page 209)** or top the Live Burrito **(page 199)** with it.

Patenada

2 cups soaked **sun-dried tomatoes**
1 cup of pitted, **sun-dried olives**
2 Tbsp. **flax seed oil**
2 Tbsp. **lemon juice**
1 tsp. **curry powder**
1/8 tsp. **cayenne pepper**

Process all the ingredients in a food processor. If you choose to use a Champion juicer, process the sun-dried tomatoes with the olives first, place in a bowl, and add the rest of the ingredients. Serve with flax crackers **(page 209)** or fresh vegetables.

CHAPTER 24: GOURMET SUNFOOD CUISINE

It is great to eat simple food. Making a meal out of plain raw fruits and vegetables can be satisfying and refreshing. Once we know that we can live on these foods, there is no more pressure to spend endless hours in the kitchen cooking. We can have more free time to do what we enjoy, and spend less time cleaning dirty pots and pans.

However, many people truly enjoy cooking and making gourmet food. These people often think that they would not be able to enjoy the **Sunfood Lifestyle**. Perhaps this is because they do not realize that it is possible to spend just as much time in the kitchen making gourmet raw food, using fruits, vegetables, nuts and seeds, as they would making traditional food. If you like to make gourmet food, the **Sunfood Lifestyle** will not be any deprivation!

Everyone likes delicious food. All the recipes in this book have been created to be tasteful and enjoyable, because I know that even your best resolutions will not last long if you do not enjoy what you eat. With raw fruits, vegetables, nuts and seeds, and the proper spices and equipment, you can let your imagination go wild and create truly amazing gourmet foods. Creations that will impress your friends and family. Almost any cooked meal could have its live counterpart, and it will taste better too! All you need to know is what tastes great, what texture you want to achieve, and you will be able to create amazing dishes.

You will learn a lot by trying the recipes in this book. The next time you open a recipe book, think about how you could make the same foods using only live ingredients. Use the same spices, and try to achieve the same texture with what you have learned in this book.

Experiment. Realize that you cannot go wrong with **The Sunfood Cuisine**. When you cook food anything can happen. If you heat something for too long, it may burn and ruin your meal. In **The Sunfood Cuisine**, you do not have to deal with heating things at the right temperature. Probably the worst that can go wrong is that you add too much of an ingredient. If this happens, do not worry. Improvise by using your concoction as a condiment for other meals!

You will find by trying the recipes in this book that **The Sunfood Cuisine** goes much further than eating plain fruits and vegetables. Food is meant to be enjoyed every day as a celebration. No one has to give up the pleasure of eating in order to become healthy.

Supreme Exotic Wild Rice Salad

3 cups sprouted **wild rice ****
1 1/2 cups **tomato**, chopped
1/4 cup **olive oil**
1 **lemon,** juice of
1 cup mashed **avocado**
1/3 cup **orange juice**
1/2 cup **cilantro** (or parsley), chopped
2 Tbsp. soaked **raisins**
1 inch grated **ginger**
2 Tbsp. of **honey** diluted with 1 Tbsp. water (optional)
1/2 to 1 tsp. **sea salt** (to taste)
2 Tbsp. **nama shoyu**, or tamari sauce

Mix all ingredients in a bowl. This is one of my favorite dishes to bring to potlucks and family gatherings. This recipe is perfect for introducing people to raw cuisine. Makes 4-5 servings.

** For this recipe, as well as with all the wild rice recipes, you will have to sprout the wild rice in advance. The technique is explained on **page 102**.

Greek Wild Rice

4 cups sprouted **wild rice ****
1/4 cup **olive oil**
1/4 cup **tahini**
4 Tbsp. **nama shoyu**, or tamari sauce
20 **green olives**, sliced
1/2 tsp. **sea salt**
1 cup **tomato**, chopped
1/2 cup **arugula**
2 **limes,** juice of
2 **garlic cloves**, minced

Pour sprouted wild rice into a bowl. In a separate bowl, add the olive oil, tahini and nama shoyu or tamari sauce, stirring into a sauce. Add to the wild rice, along with the rest of the ingredients. Serve with green salad. Serves 4-5. **The technique is explained on **page 102**.

Pad Thai

2 cups **cucumber spirals** **
6 cups **angel hair pasta (page 200)**
2 cups **purple cabbage**, shredded

Place in two to four individual bowls. *** Use the Saladacco machine, with the function that makes big spirals, not the small pasta-like ones. If you do not have this tool you can slice the vegetables very thin, lengthwise, or use a vegetable peeler.*

Sauce:
4 Tbsp. **tahini**
2 Tbsp. **almond butter**
2 medium **avocados**, mashed **
1/2 cup **orange juice**
1 tsp. **curry powder**
4 Tbsp. **nama shoyu**, or tamari sauce
cayenne pepper, to taste

Mix everything together in a bowl. Serve sauce on top of vegetables.

** You can mash them in the sauce bowl. They should not be entirely liquefied.

Add as garnish:
4 Tbsp. **onions**, diced
1/2 cup **red or yellow peppers**, diced
1/2 cup **marinated mushrooms (see page 206)**

Place the pasta in individual bowls. Add sauce, and distribute the garnish evenly. Serves 2-4.

Live Burrito

purple cabbage leaves
your favorite **guacamole** recipe

Stuff guacamole inside the purple cabbage leaves. Eat like a burrito.
This is one of my favorite quick meals.

Variation: Try with romaine lettuce leaves, or with a different dip inside.

Angel Hair Pasta

To create angel hair pasta, you will need to use the Saladacco/Spiralizer. As you probably already know, the machine has two positions, one that makes thin spirals, and one that makes large spirals. You will use the thinner position to make angel hair pasta. You will need to cut pieces that are not too big, but not too small either. Find the perfect size, which fills the most space possible.

You can make pasta out of:

zucchini (my favorite because of the texture),
carrot, beet, sweet potato, squash
turnip, yams, and **butternut squash**.

Serve with your favorite raw pasta sauce.
(Can also be served with any dressings)

San Diego Pasta

Pasta:

8 cups <u>Angel Hair Pasta</u>, (above)
(two-thirds zucchini, and one-third cucumber)

Place the pasta into a bowl. You can also make the pasta by slicing the vegetables very thin, or peeling the zucchini with a vegetable peeler, until there is almost nothing left, and omit the cucumber.

Place in a bowl, and cut across with a knife a couple times — or else you may find yourself with ten-foot-long pasta strips!

Sauce:

1/4 cup **olive oil**
2 cups **tomato**, diced
1 cup **parsley**, chopped
1 cup **arugula**, chopped
4 Tbsp. **tahini**, diluted with 4 Tbsp. of water in a bowl
4 Tbsp. **nama shoyu**, or tamari sauce
pinch of **sea salt**
1/4 cup **olives**, pitted and chopped
2 **avocados**, diced
4 **green onions**, chopped
pinch of **black pepper**

Mix everything in a bowl. Add on top of the pasta. Serves 2-4.

Pasta al Frédéric

Pasta:
6 cups Angel Hair Pasta, made with **zucchini (see page 200)**

   Place in a bowl, then add

1 1/2 cup diced **tomatoes**

Sauce:
1/4 cup **tahini**
1/4 cup **olive oil**
1/2 tsp. **cumin**
1/2 tsp. **oregano**
1 **lime** or lemon, juice of
1 Tbsp. **apple cider vinegar**
2 Tbsp. **nama shoyu**, or tamari sauce
1 tsp. red **miso**

   Mix all ingredients with a spoon in a bowl, or use a blender.
   Mix in with the pasta. Sprinkle with chopped arugula or dill. Serves 2-3.

Pasta Marinara

Pasta:
6 cups Angel Hair Pasta, made with zucchini **(see page 200)**

Sauce:
1/4 cup **lime juice**
1/4 cup **olive oil**
1 **garlic clove**, minced
1/4 cup **cilantro**, chopped
1/4 cup **fresh dill** (or basil), chopped
2 Tbsp. **nama shoyu**, or tamari sauce
1/4 cup **green olives** (or kalamata), pitted and chopped
1 cup **tomato**, diced
1 pinch **black pepper** (optional)
1 pinch **cayenne pepper** (optional)

   Mix all the sauce ingredients, except the pepper and cayenne, directly in
   with the pasta. Sprinkle with pepper and cayenne, if desired. Serves 2-3.

Real Spaghetti

Pasta:

8 cups <u>Angel Hair Pasta</u>, made with zucchini and cucumber
(two-thirds zucchini, and one-third cucumber).

Serve topped with <u>Better Than Mom's Tomato Sauce</u> (following recipe).
It looks similar to spaghetti, and tastes better. Also, this recipe
is entirely made out of vegetables… not a drop of oil is used!

Better Than Mom's Tomato Sauce

3 cups **tomato**, diced
4 Tbsp. **apple cider vinegar**
1 Tbsp. **honey**, or 2-3 dates
1/2 to 3/4 tsp. **sea salt** (to taste)
1 Tbsp. **Italian herb mix** (a mix of basil, thyme, oregano, and garlic)
1/2 cup **fresh basil**, or 2 Tbsp. dried
1 1/2 cups **sun-dried tomatoes**
1 tsp. **jalapeño pepper**
1 medium **garlic clove**

Blend until smooth. If you do not have a Vita-Mix, you will need to
soak the sun-dried tomatoes in water beforehand. Soak them for a few
hours, then discard the soak water. Makes 2 cups.

Chile Sin Cocción

2 cups either **chopped broccoli, cauliflower, purple cabbage**,
   or a combination of all three
2 Tbsp. **onion**, chopped
2 cups **zucchini**, sliced into strips
1 cup **red bell pepper**, diced
1 cup <u>Better Than Mom's Tomato Sauce</u>
   (recipe above)
1-2 tsp. **chili powder**

Mix all ingredients in a bowl.
Add more or less chili powder
depending on your taste.
Serves 3-4.

Butternut Squash Spaghetti

4 cups <u>Angel Hair Pasta</u> **made out of butternut squash (see page 200)**
1 cup <u>Angel Hair Pasta</u> **made with zucchini (see page 200)**
4 Tbsp. **olive oil**
2 Tbsp. **apple cider vinegar**
1/2 **lemon**, juice of
1/4 to 1/2 tsp. **sea salt** (to taste)
1 cup **parsley**, chopped
1/2 medium **tomato**, chopped

Using the Saladacco, spiralize the long, peeled neck of a butternut squash, cutting pieces of a size that can fit into the machine. When you have about 3 cups of butternut squash pasta, make another cup of zucchini pasta. Place in a big bowl. Cut through the pasta a few times with a knife to avoid having spirals that are too long. Add the remaining ingredients, mix well, and let sit a few hours before serving. (If you can wait that long…)

Raw Hummus

2 cups soaked **almonds**
1/2 cup **tahini**
1 large **garlic clove**, minced
2 large **lemons**, juice of
1/3 cup **olive oil**
1/4 to 1/2 tsp. **sea salt** (to taste)

Homogenize the almonds using your Champion or Green Power juicer with the blank plate. Add into a food processor along with all the other ingredients. Try to achieve a smooth consistency, adding some water if necessary. Serve with green vegetables such as lettuce, cabbage, and kale.

Cherry tomato

Nori Rolls

sun-dried **nori sheets**
your favorite **pâté** recipe **(page 182)**
avocado pieces, or guacamole recipe **(page 190)** or hummus recipe **(page 203)**
shredded **carrots**, or beets
shredded **zucchini**, or cabbage
long, thin sticks of **cucumber**
alfalfa or clover sprouts, or shredded lettuce

OPTIONAL:
sun-dried tomatoes (previously soaked in water for a few hours)
pitted olives
pickled ginger (available in most health food stores)

Place all of the ingredients, except the nori, in separate bowls. Set up your working space nicely. Have a bowl of water and a sharp knife. Have a dry cutting board. Place one sheet of nori on the cutting board, horizontally facing you. First spread a couple of spoonfuls of pâté onto the horizontal half of the nori sheet that is facing you. Spread evenly. Do not put too much, just a thin, but nice, spread. Add a couple pieces of avocado, or a couple spoonfuls of guacamole or hummus. Add a few sun-dried tomatoes, and a few pieces of olives, and pickled ginger if desired. Add a small amount of shredded vegetables, enough to cover everything. Add one stick of cucumber, and a small amount of sprouts, or lettuce. Roll the nori like a cigar. Some people like to roll the sushi using a sushi mat. I do not like using such mats, but if you do, you can use them. To seal the sushi, put a little water on the edge before you finish rolling it. Cut into small, bite-sized pieces. Rinse your knife between each cut. The key here is too cut very slowly, to avoid tearing the nori.

Try not to make your Nori Rolls too thick. If they are so big that they could not be eaten in one bite, it is because you are putting too many ingredients inside. You will soon find the ideal proportions.

You may also make nori rolls with only avocados, and no nut pâté. This is how I usually like them. Use 1/2 avocado per nori roll.

Everyone loves these nori rolls. Serve on a plate. You can also serve a Nori Roll Sauce to dip them in **(page 205)**.

Nori Roll Sauce

one part **water**
one part **nama shoyu**, or tamari sauce
powdered ginger

> In a bowl, mix nama shoyu and water together. The quantity you need depends on how many sushi rolls you have. Sprinkle with a bit of ginger.

Quick Nori Rolls

1 **nori sheet**
1/2 **avocado**
1/2 **lime,** juice of
1/2 to 1 cup **lettuce**
1 tsp. **olive oil**
1 pinch **sea salt**
nama shoyu, or tamari sauce (to taste)

> Spread the avocado on half of the nori sheet. Squeeze lime on top. Add olive oil, lettuce, sea salt, and nama shoyu. Roll it up (do not cut it) and eat.

La Salade de Robert

3 to 4 medium **apples**
2 **celery stalks**
10-15 **green olives**
1 cup **almond mayonnaise** or avocado mayonnaise **(see page 193)**
1/2 tsp. **cumin**

> Peel, core and slice apples super thin. Then cut these apple slices in two or three. Slice the celery and green olives finely. Put everything into a bowl. Mix with almond mayonnaise, and sprinkle with the cumin. This is a raw version of a favorite dish of my grandfather, who had a long career as a French chef. Serves 3-4.

Portobello Supreme

portobello mushroom caps, with the base recipe of <u>Super Guac</u> **(page 190)**

> Top the mushrooms with as much <u>Super Guac</u> as you can. Devour without guilt. If you do not have guacamole ready, simply mash an avocado on top of each mushroom, add a little garlic-oil, lemon juice, sea salt, and nama shoyu or tamari sauce. This makes great "fast food."

Eggplant Lasagna

1 medium to large **eggplant**
2 cups **water**
1/4 cup **nama shoyu**, or tamari sauce
1 tsp. **sea salt**

Cut eggplant thin lengthwise. Marinate in water, nama shoyu or tamari sauce and sea salt for at least 2 hours, and up to 12 hours. Dry the eggplant slices with a paper towel.

Prepare the following in separate bowls:

1 cup Better Than Mom's Tomato Sauce **(page 202)**
2 cups shredded **zucchini**
a few slices of **red onion**

Cheese sauce:
1/3 cup **tahini**
1/3 cup **olive oil**
2 Tbsp. **nama shoyu**, or tamari sauce

Mix together in a bowl until smooth.

Create different layers, alternating:
Eggplant, tomato sauce, shredded zucchini, cheese sauce, eggplant, tomato sauce, etc. Finish with shredded zucchini, and decorate with a few slices of onion. Serves 2-4.

Marinated Mushrooms

1/2 cup **nama shoyu**, or tamari sauce
1/2 cup **water**
2 cups sliced or diced **mushrooms** (portobello, white mushrooms, or others)
1/3 cup **olive oil**
garlic powder (optional)

In a bowl, mix the nama shoyu or tamari sauce, water, and olive oil together. Add the mushrooms and let marinate for 1 to 8 hours. Drain the marinade, and save it for future use. Sprinkle with garlic powder if desired.

Tostadas

Flax Seed Crackers **(page 209)**
Super Guac, or your favorite guacamole recipe **(page 190)**
Mango Salsa, or your favorite salsa recipe **(page 192)**

Top flax crackers with guacamole and salsa. Enjoy with sides of lettuce, and slices of tomatoes and cucumbers.

Jícama Salad

4 cups **jícama**, diced
2 **green onions**, chopped
4 Tbsp. **tahini**
1 **lemon**, juice of
2 Tbsp. **apple cider vinegar**
3 Tbsp. **nama shoyu** (or tamari sauce)
1 pinch **black pepper**
1 tsp. **Italian herb mix**
   (a mix of basil, thyme, oregano, and garlic)

Place diced jicama in a bowl, along with the green onions. In another bowl, make a sauce of the remaining ingredients using your fork to make it smooth. Mix with the jícama, then serve. Serves 2-3.

Raw Thai Stir-Live

4 cups **purple cabbage**, chopped
2 cups **cauliflower**, chopped
1 **yellow** (or red) **bell pepper**, chopped
2 cups **white mushrooms**, sliced
1/2 cup **cilantro**, chopped
1/2 cup **tomato**, chopped
1 **avocado**, diced
1-2 inches **ginger**, grated
2 medium **garlic cloves**, minced
1 Tbsp. **lemon zest ****
4 Tbsp. **nama shoyu** (or tamari sauce)
1/4 cup **olive oil**
1 pinch **cayenne pepper**, or 1/4 tsp. jalapeño pepper
2 Tbsp. **honey**, diluted in 1 Tbsp. water

Mix all ingredients. Serves 4.
** Lemon zest is lemon peel that has been shredded.

Salade de la Mer

2 cups **arame**
water, for soaking arame
4 cups **carrots**, shredded
2 Tbsp. **olive oil**
1 **garlic clove**, minced (optional)
2 Tbsp. **nama shoyu** (or tamari sauce)
2 Tbsp. **apple cider vinegar**
1 **lemon**, juice of
1 **avocado**, smashed in a bowl by using a fork
1/2 to 1 tsp. **sea salt** (to taste)

First soak the arame. Cover with water and let soak for about 15 to 20 minutes. It will double in volume. Then drain the soaking water, and rinse the arame well. Mix with all the other ingredients in a bowl. Serve Japanese style with chop sticks, accompanied with Nori Rolls **(page 204).**
Serves 3-4.

DEHYDRATOR RECIPES:

Basic Flax Cracker Recipe

2 cups **flax seeds**
2 cups **water**
2 Tbsp. **nama shoyu** (or tamari sauce), or 1/2 tsp. sea salt (optional)

Soak flax seeds in water for at least 30 minutes, and up to 6 hours. Mix with sea salt or nama shoyu. Add more or less according to your taste. Spread on dehydrator sheets (Teflex sheets), and dehydrate for about 8 hours. For your convenience, you may make them at night, and dehydrate them overnight. When they are completely dry, break apart into cracker-sized pieces, and eat with soups, guacamole, etc.

Mexican Flax Crackers

2 cups **flax seeds**
2 cups **water**
1 1/2 cups **tomato**, finely diced
2-3 tsp. **chile powder**
1/2 to 1 tsp. **sea salt** (to taste)

Soak flax seeds in water for at least 30 minutes, and up to 6 hours. Mix with the rest of the ingredients in a bowl. Use more or less chili powder according to your taste. Spread on dehydrator sheets (Teflex sheets), and dehydrate for about 8 hours. For your convenience, you may make them at night and dehydrate overnight. When they are completely dry, break apart into cracker-sized pieces, and eat with soups, guacamole, and pâtés.

Curried Flax Crackers

2 cups **flax seeds**
2 cups **water**
2 Tbsp. **curry powder**
2 Tbsp. **nama shoyu**, or tamari sauce
1/4-1/2 tsp. **sea salt** (to taste)
1 **lemon**, juice of

Preparation: same method as for previous crackers.

Italian Flax Crackers

2 cups **flax seeds**
2 cups **water**
2 medium **garlic cloves**, minced
1 tsp. **dried basil**
1 tsp. **dried oregano**
1/2 tsp. **dried sage**
1/2 tsp. **dried marjoram**
1 cup **tomato**, chopped
1/4 cup **tomato powder** **
1 **lemon,** juice of
1/2 to 1 tsp. **sea salt** (to taste)

Preparation: Same method as for previous crackers.

** Tomato powder is made out of sun-dried tomatoes, and can be found in some health food stores. If this ingredient is not available, you can skip it.

Nori Sticks

4 to 5 **nori sheets**
2 cups soaked **sunflower seeds**
4 Tbsp. **nama shoyu,** or tamari sauce
1 Tbsp. **Italian herb mix** (a mix of basil, thyme, oregano, and garlic)
1/2 **lemon**, juice of

Make a pâté out of the last four ingredients. Run the sunflower seeds through a Champion or Green Power juicer (with the blank plate on), or blend in a Vita-Mix. If using the Vita-Mix, mix all the ingredients in the container before blending. Otherwise, run the sunflower seeds through the Champion (or Green Life/Green Power), place in a bowl, then mix in with the rest of the ingredients. Next, cut the nori sheets in half, where they naturally fold. Use about two tablespoons of nut pâté per half nori sheet. Spread on half of this cut sheet, and roll up. Seal with a little water. Dehydrate these "sticks" for 8-12 hours. You can also vary this recipe using any other nut pâté.

Mock-Salmon Burgers

2 cups soaked **almonds**
2 medium **carrots**
1 **lemon,** juice of
1/2 Tbsp. **sea salt**
1 Tbsp. **Italian herb mix** (a mix of basil, thyme, oregano, and garlic)
1/2 small **red onion**

Puree the almonds and carrots using your Champion/Green Power juicer with the blank plate on. Place the mixture in a bowl, then add the other ingredients. Mix well. Form 6-8 "burgers," and dehydrate at 100 degrees Fahrenheit, for 6-8 hours. Place the burgers on Teflex sheets before dehydrating, and turn them over after 3-4 hours.

CHAPTER 25: SUNFOOD SNACKS

Often the best meals are simple recipes put together on the spot. What is great about the **Sunfood Diet** is that it is possible to eat that way all the time, with no time involved in lengthy preparation. Occasionally, we like to make something more gourmet, but as time is often against us, it is great to know that we do not have to spend any extra time in the kitchen to eat healthy. Here are some recipe ideas that can be put together in a few minutes. I am sure you will come up with your own, as you realize how tasty raw fruits and vegetables are in their natural state. You often have to combine only two or three ingredients to create something delicious.

Almond Butter-Apples

Slice some apples. Spread almond butter on them, then eat.

Avocado-Olives

Mash an avocado in a bowl. Add chopped, pitted olives, and mix well with some lemon juice.

Avocado-Dulse

Rinse some whole leaf dulse. Chop, then place in a bowl. Mash an avocado, then mix this with the dulse.

Avocado-Romaine Lettuce

Wrap pieces of avocado inside lettuce leaves, then eat as a "raw burrito."

Romaine-Tahini-Dulse

Wrap pieces of avocado inside a leaf of romaine lettuce, add some dulse, then spread some tahini on top. Eat like a sandwich.

Avocado-Kale-Dates

Eat avocado, kale, and dates, one bite of each at a time.

Macadamia-Apricots

Eat macadamia nuts with some apricots. This combination tastes buttery and sweet.

Tomato-Dulse

Dice a tomato and place in a bowl. Add some rinsed, chopped dulse, then drizzle with olive oil.

Hazelnuts-Raisins

Make a trail mix by combining hazelnuts with raisins.

Lettuce-Bananas

Wrap a small banana inside a romaine lettuce leaf, then eat as a sandwich. Sweet variation: top the banana with some tahini and honey.

Cabbage-Avocado

Wrap pieces of avocado inside a cabbage leaf, then eat as a sandwich.

Cabbage-Tahini-Dulse-Lemon

Spread some tahini inside a cabbage leaf. Add some chopped, rinsed dulse, then drizzle with lemon juice. Roll, and eat.

Wild Greens-Cabbage-Avocado

Find some wild, edible greens that grow in your area. You can find about them in a book titled **Edible Wild Plants: a North American Field Guide**. Place inside a cabbage leaf along with some avocado, then eat as a sandwich.

Chile Peppers-Avocado

Eat hot chile peppers and avocado together.

Durian-Friend

Find a good durian at your nearest Asian market. Eat with a friend!

Red Bell Pepper-Basil-Avocado

Place some mashed avocado inside half a seeded red bell pepper, then top with some basil leaf.

Avocado-Spirulina Flakes

Mash some avocado in a bowl with spirulina flakes and lemon juice. Eat with a spoon. Variation: add miso.

Date-Almond Candies

Pit several dates, then replace the pit with an almond. Serve as candies.

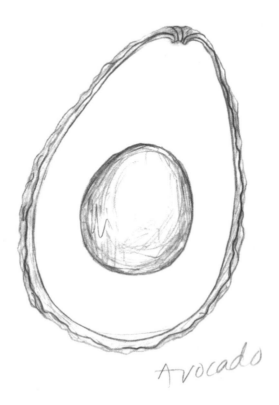

Avocado

APPENDIX 1:
HOW TO TRANSITION TO A HEALTHY LIFESTYLE

Everyone is at a different stage in their dietary evolution. I wrote this book so that everyone, no matter where they are, can benefit from it. I do not condemn you if you still eat meat, dairy products, ice cream, sugar, and the other things that you know are less than excellent for your health. My job is not to make you feel guilty. Buying this book is proof that you are on your way to a better diet. Reading this book shows that you are interested in having more fruits and vegetables on your plate, less of the cooked and processed foods, and a more vibrant and healthy life.

A diet high in raw foods is a challenge for many people, and most, including myself, make the change to what I call the "**Sunfood Lifestyle**" as a gradual process rather than as an overnight transformation. I will show you how you can ease into this lifestyle at a pace that is comfortable to you. I will also give you tips on how to cope with the difficulties you may encounter along the way.

First, understand that no matter what the state of your health is, you can benefit from eating more raw fruits and vegetables. Some people will feel that they are ready to eat all uncooked vegan foods, while others will gradually work their way into a healthier lifestyle. They will do this by eating more and more of the good foods, and less and less of the cooked and processed foods. We often hear about percentages to determine the level of commitment one has to a raw-vegan lifestyle. Some say, "I'm 80% raw," or "I eat 100% raw," meaning that 80% or 100% of what they eat is uncooked and unprocessed. These percentages reflect how far a person has decided to go with the **Sunfood Diet**.

The first step to becoming a raw-vegan is obviously to eat more raw foods. Everyone should be eating at least 50% to 70% raw fruits and vegetables, no matter where they live, or what they do. Eating 50% to 70% raw fruits and vegetables is easier than you might think. As explained in the book **Fit for Life**, one should partake of fruits and/or juices in the morning. Because the body has been in an elimination period during the night, it is better not to stress the body with heavy food in the morning. So by eating healthy every morning, your body can continue the job of elimination that it was busy doing during the night.

It is good to start the day by drinking water. I suggest drinking at least 10-20 ounces of water with some fresh lemon juice every morning. This will hydrate your body, and help flush out the toxins that have been eliminated from the cells during the night. It will also help the body to eliminate. Make sure that the water you drink is pure. Either purified, distilled, or a good-quality bottled water. When possible, get your water in glass bottles. Glass is cleaner, and does not carry any of the toxic components that plastic does. You can also get for about $30 a water purifier which will remove 98% of the toxic materials from tap water.

After you have your morning water, you may have some healthy beverages, such as freshly pressed juice. Have only liquids within the first two to three hours after waking. This will give your body a rest, and leave your mind clear and fresh.

Later in the morning, you may have some fruit if you feel hungry. Do not limit the quantity of fruit that you need to eat in order to satisfy your hunger. Eat as much as you want. You may eat two or three apples if you want. Most people are used to eating one apple once in a while. However, if you are to make a meal out of fruit only, you can eat more than one piece. Your taste buds will tell you when you have had enough of any one food.

For lunch, have a salad with avocado or some nuts. If you are eating cooked food, have only one kind and eat it with a salad. Always eat raw vegetables every time you eat cooked food. Have the salad first, and then have whatever else you want. If you must hve cooked food, have only one type, like a rice dish, some bread, or a soup. If you feel satisfied with your salad meal, why eat something else that would be less than excellent? Get on with your day. If you do not feel like having anything cooked for lunch, but do not feel totally satisfied with your salad, have something heavier. In addition to your salad, you could have guacamole, or other raw dips. Or maybe bring along a nut pâté, or simply some nuts and seeds to munch on. Also, olives can be very satisfying as a lunch-time snack.

During the rest of the day, eat fruit or raw vegetables when you feel like munching on something. Try to reduce your consumption of hot beverages, such as tea and coffee. Instead, drink more water. You may also try bringing a mix of nuts, seeds, and dried fruits as a snack to work.

For dinner, when you are home, make yourself a living soup and/or a salad. Experiment with some of the recipes in this book. You may accompany your meal with salad. If you feel like having an all raw meal, you could have guacamole, or nut pâté in a "burrito" (inside a lettuce or cabbage leaf).

If you still eat cooked food, but eat fruit in the morning, and a salad with every meal, plus have fruits and vegetables as snacks, you will be eating 50-70% raw, with almost no effort! Eating that way is both easy, and healthy. And you will enjoy it too. Prepare great dressings in advance and bring them along with you to work. When you make a recipe from **The Sunfood Cuisine**, make extra, and save some to bring with you to work. If you do not have time to prepare a meal in advance, then bring some raw fruits and vegetables along with nuts and seeds. Also, you can bring an avocado along with you, and eat it with a spoon, or add it to a salad at a restaurant. Many people bring their own salad dressings with them when they eat at restaurants.

Get in the habit of eating an abundance of raw fruits and vegetables. Eat lettuce and celery with everything. Bring carrot sticks with you in a plastic bag. Just get the raw food in! That is the first step. If you desire a beverage, make yourself a great juice in the morning. Apple-celery juice is a good choice. For dinner, start your meal with a green drink. Eat salad as a meal whenever possible. Experiment with fruits and vegetables you have never tried. Go to the market and get exotic fruits. Buy a new fruit or vegetable every week. Experiment with the variety Nature offers. Get your taste buds back into shape. Once you start eating more fruits and vegetables, they will become what you truly desire to eat. By filling your body with good nutrition, you will feel much better, and your body will request more.

After introducing better foods into your diet, you can start eliminating what is not healthy. The first type of food you want to avoid is processed food. Processed food is anything that comes in a can or from a factory, and contains additives and preservatives. It is also all the junk food that is served at the popular snack bars. So become health conscious, and refuse to eat refined sugar, refined flour, table salt, and foods that contain additives and/or preservatives. Stop shopping at the supermarket, and start shopping at the health food store. Buy organic food, and avoid anything that has been refined or processed in a food factory.

Other foods to be avoided are animal products and cooked starches. Animal products include fish, chicken, beef, and pork, as well as dairy products such as milk, cheese, yogurt, and eggs. The consumption of animal products has been shown to be related to a variety of diseases, including cancer, heart disease, and diabetes. If you need a more in-depth explanation of what eating animals does to your health and the planet, I suggest reading the book, **Diet For A New America**, by John Robbins.

Many people in America are now becoming vegetarians for various reasons, health being one of them. It is known that, on average, vegetarians live longer than meat eaters, and experience fewer diseases. A vegetarian diet can do a lot for you, when it is practiced correctly. Vegetarians are becoming a part of the mainstream society, and most restaurants now carry vegetarian options. If none are listed, ask - they will frequently make one for you. Many people try to cut down on their meat intake, as they are learning about what a plant-based diet can do for them.

The downfall of the vegetarian diet is the high amount of cooked starches it often contains. Cooked starches include cooked grains and legumes, as well as the food items made from them such as bread, pasta, cookies, and crackers. It also includes baked potatoes. Most vegetarians eat a lot of these foods and, as a result, are not experiencing a high level of vitality. Many of the new diets in vogue these days, such as the Zone diet, promote fewer cooked starches (also called "carbohydrates"). Why? Because many people have found that eating cooked starches makes you gain weight, and may cause or aggravate many health conditions.

The trick to reducing, and eventually eliminating, the amount of starches you are eating is to eat starches no more than once or twice per day, and have only one type of starch at a meal. If you are going to have bread, then have bread, but not bread, potatoes, and rice. Also, there are some cooked starches that are easier on the body than others. Cooked sweet potatoes, or yams, for example, are a better choice than white potatoes. Brown rice is better than white rice. Sprouted bread is better than regular bread. Wheat products tend to be the worst type of cooked starch for many people. Wheat is a common allergen, and many find great relief in eliminating wheat products from their diet.

The last category of foods to reduce are all the other cooked and processed foods. This includes all the cooked vegetables, stewed fruits, and other cooked items. We have already discussed the issue of refined foods, so I am not going to talk here about all the condiments (ketchup, mustard, etc.), canned foods, and heavily processed and refined foods that you already avoid, and know to be bad for you. So that just leaves us with anything else that has been heated or processed.

Few people go as far as to eliminate all cooked foods from their diet, and for many it would seem an impossible goal that they would never be able to achieve. Many people would view such a move as quite radical and extreme. Yet, thousands of people throughout the world every year are learning about the benefits of eating raw plant foods, and deciding to let go of all cooked and processed foods. There will be a point in your dietary evolution where you will decide if you are ready to take this step. When this happens, just relax, let go, and embrace your new and fresh raw-vegan lifestyle. Nature will welcome you back into the world of pure and simple eating.

For those who are not ready to make such a move, or who feel it is not time for them, they can still benefit from increasing the amount of raw fruits and vegetables they are eating. They will still eat cooked foods, perhaps only on some occasions, but far less with every month that passes. For these people, we recommend cooked vegetables as the best choice of cooked food to eat. Starchless cooked vegetables, such as steamed kale, broccoli, spinach, zucchini, celery, cauliflower, peppers, and other vegetables, are quite healthy in comparison to cooked starches. Cooked or baked sweet potatoes (yams) are a more healthy food to eat than baked white potatoes.

When eating cooked foods, always eat a salad or other raw foods. If you bake a sweet potato, mash it in a bowl with some avocado, olive oil, and other seasonings. When eating steamed vegetables, top them with one of the salad dressings in this book or with any of the raw dips and raw sauces that you enjoy. Get the raw in with everything that you eat!

RAW FOODS IN THE WINTER

Another challenge that many people face when eating a raw-vegan diet is maintaining the lifestyle during the cold winters. Winter, for many of us, equals snow, cold, and a reduced variety of fresh fruits and vegetables available in the stores. Many people are used to drinking warm soups and other hot foods in the winter to stay warm, and feel that it would be hard for them to eat mainly raw foods during that time of the year.

First, it is good to know that eating hot foods will not necessarily make you warm. They will give you the illusion of being warm. Eating foods at room temperature will not necessarily make you feel cold, as long as you do not eat freezing foods, or fruit straight out of the fridge. The temperature of the food, in reality, has little effect on the ability of your body to produce internal heat. There are millions of animals living in the wild on Earth, eating only raw foods during the cold winter, and every one of them can handle the cold better than any of us so-called civilized humans. Would they be better off eating hot foods? I don't think so.

Meanwhile, we are not living with the animals in the wild, but in cities where things are quite different. Although our living conditions may be different than those of wild animals, our physiology is not. We are still bound by the same natural laws. As you improve your health with your diet, you should be able to withstand the cold much better, and will lose your desire for hot foods. It is possible that you might feel colder in the first months of your change of diet, as your body is adjusting and releasing toxins. But after a while, you will find that you can resist the cold much better.

In the winter time, I understand that warm foods such as soup may be comforting and enjoyable. If you would like to have a warm soup, here is a recipe that may help you:

Warm miso soup
2 cups **water**
2 Tbsp. **miso**
Small pinch of **sea salt**
pinch of **cayenne pepper**
1 **garlic clove**
1/2 cup of your **favorite herb**, such as cilantro, parsley, or dill. (Optional)
2 Tbsp. **olive oil**

> Blend all ingredients except olive oil at high speed for a few seconds, and then pour into a pot. Warm up to desired temperature (keep under 110 degrees Fahrenheit). Add olive oil, mix well, and enjoy.

You can also warm up any of the soup recipes in this book, if you feel you want to have something hot. You do not have to cook them, but just warm them up. It is much better to have something warm that is liquid, rather than a hot meal that is heavy. Liquid foods are always easier on the digestive organs.

Also, in order to go through the winter easier on a raw-vegan diet, there are a few other things you may want to try. One of them is to get some sunshine. I know that sun is scarce in the winter, but it is possible to get some sun on your skin. Exposure to even weak sun is great for your immune system, and enables you to go through the winter with more facility. The lack of sunshine during the winter causes many people to feel depressed. Some people have named this condition the "winter blues." To avoid this, get some sun on your skin regularly. You can stand naked behind a window when the sun shines through. Another way is to engage in outdoor activities. The sun tends to reflect greatly on the snow, and people often get sunburned while going skiing. You will benefit from limited exposure to the sun. Try to get the sun on your face, your hands, and as much of your body as you can safely and conveniently expose.

Exercise is a great way to fight the "SAD" winter blues (SAD: Seasonal Associated Depression/Seasonal Affective Disorder). There are many types of outdoor exercises that can be enjoyed during the winter, such as going for a brisk walk, or skiing. Don't get lazy because it is cold... keep going with your exercise program, and if you do not have one, think about starting one. If you can take time, go outside and play on the weekends. Also, keep exercising indoors by engaging in cardiovascular and resistance training.

Dr. Kristine Nolfi, who wrote **Raw Food Treatment of Cancer**, said that fruits and vegetables carry within them the sun's energy. She said that when a person eats a diet based on fruits and vegetables, they go through the winter without getting sick, and with much more ease and enjoyment. She was living in Denmark, where she had a successful retreat center treating people using raw fruits and vegetables. We should all listen to her advice, and understand how powerful these foods are for us. Many people eat a terrible diet during the winter, often eating foods that are totally devoid of life. Without the proper vitamins and nutrients, the immune system cannot function properly. Then these people get sick and wonder why. If they were to base their diet on fruits and vegetables, they would find that they would not get sick so often, even during the winter. They would go through the winter months with perfect enjoyment and ease.

By eating raw fruits and vegetables, exercising, and getting some sunshine, you will breeze through the winter with ease, and may even find yourself looking forward to the next winter. You can view winter as a time of cold, isolation, and boredom, or as a time of excitement, fun, and magic! Remember, how much you enjoy life has a lot to do with your selected perspective.

DETOXIFICATION PROCESS

As you improve your diet, it is inevitable that you will go through a healing process. Just like the smoker who stops smoking and proceeds to experience headaches and other discomforts, after you start following a cleaner diet, you go through what we call "detoxification." On a conventional diet, toxins accumulate in the body faster than they can be eliminated. The body, not being able to cope with all this toxic assault, stores these toxins in various places, with the intention to eliminate them later. When you improve your diet by eating less and by eating lighter foods, there is more body energy available. Digestion takes a lot of energy, and when you are eating heavy foods, such as bread and meat, a lot of this energy that your body has at its disposal is used to digest these heavy foods. When you eat a diet based on raw fruits and vegetables, you are freeing much of that burden, since these foods are easy to digest, and also due to the fact that you are bringing less toxins into the body.

Fruits and vegetables when eaten raw contain fewer toxins than cooked and processed foods. They also contain plenty of vitamins, minerals, and other nutritional components that your body can use to heal and maintain itself.

Someone said, "You have to feel worse before you can feel better!" This is often true. We cannot expect to eat junk food for decades, suddenly stop all of that, and then instantly feel better. Our bodies, when given the chance to heal and detoxify, will use that opportunity to get all of the garbage out.

To learn more about the process of detoxification, you should read David Wolfe's book, **The Sunfood Diet Success System**, which goes into great detail on how to deal with conditions that may be experienced while the body is eliminating toxins. After you have improved your diet, remember to be easy with yourself. If you feel low one day, rest more and do something you enjoy. Keep your smile, and know that these discomforts are only temporary, and soon you will feel much better. Also, by spending more time outside and exercising, you will hasten the process of detoxification.

DEALING WITH FRIENDS AND FAMILY

When confronted with friends and family, a good attitude to have is to not try to convert everyone around you. Confronting someone about their diet is taboo, because people do not like to be told that what they are eating is unhealthy. They certainly do not want to be told what to eat. So do not try to convince anyone. Simply go on with your life. People who are interested in what you are doing will come to you. Then you can give them a book, and answer their questions. But, unless someone comes to you for guidance, there is no reason to try to convince anyone.

You do not have to talk about your diet. You do not have to tell anyone what you are doing. When you are invited somewhere, bring along your own food, and eat whatever healthy option they have for you. If they ask you questions, just say that you are on a special diet.

Remember, the idea here is to avoid confrontation. Do not engage in conversations about diet and food every time you visit friends and family. If you are in a more relaxed situation, with people who are open and understanding, you may then share some of your experiences. If you are not totally sure about the factual aspects of the vegetarian diet, just talk about your experiences with it. Talk about the benefits, without expecting them to believe every word.

In any case, do not fall into fanaticism. As you cannot be entirely sure that what you are doing is 100% right, there is no way you can know what is right for someone else. Do not think you have all the answers. Do not even think that your diet is "better." Simply follow what you think is best for your health, and if it doesn't seem to work for you, then try something else. We are all different so there is no way of eating that can work for everyone.

I have assumed in this chapter that you are already aware of the unhealthy but common substances such as: alcohol, tobacco, drugs, caffeine, and other obvious health-sappers. I have not discussed these topics, because I feel you are probably aware of these issues.

HERE'S TO YOUR RADIANT HEALTH

Your health is your most valuable asset, and you should care for it as well as you can. Invest in the best fuel to put in it, and treat your body like you would treat your most valuable possession. See your body as a temple, and with every mouthful of food that you put in it, see it as what you choose to bring to your temple.

APPENDIX 2: HYBRID FOOD AND WILD FOOD

Agriculture has been in existence for thousands of years, and throughout that time farmers have sought ways to improve their crops. Many techniques have been invented to modify the qualities of plants. For example, wild watermelons are quite bitter and not sweet. Wild almonds are poisonous. These foods have been hybridized using various methods, so now they are edible and pleasing to the taste. The various methods used in agriculture include selection, grafting, and crossbreeding. These methods have their benefits, since they have enabled us to eat many foods that we could not otherwise eat.

Hybridization is, after all, a natural process that many animals engage in. We eat fruits that we enjoy, and tend to propagate seeds of the plants that are the most pleasing to our taste. We then reproduce more of the plants that had pleasing qualities, such as sweetness. Farmers have done nothing more than copy what was actually done in Nature, by selecting the seeds that gave the best crops, and planting those seeds for the next season, instead of the seeds from the plants that gave poor results.

The downside of all this is that plants are now hybridized for reasons other than quality and taste. Nowadays plants are hybridized for commercial reasons such as to get bigger fruits, fruits with fewer "imperfections," cold-resistant plants, and plants that have less seeds, or other features that the markets request. We create plants that might have the physical qualities we seek, but have little taste and nutrition, to the point where most fruits and vegetables grown today by traditional methods, and often even organic methods, are incredibly tasteless, as well as low in vitamins and minerals.

Walk into your nearest supermarket, and you will see the lamentable reality. Shiny round apples with no taste, tomatoes without flavor, citrus that lacks sweetness, watery grapes with a detestable after-taste, and lettuce that has to be soaked in dressing to have any flavor at all. If our ancestors were still alive, they would likely express disappointment and disgust with today's produce, having been raised on foods that came from local gardens.

Many people, because of this, revert to the methods of our great-grandparents, and start to grow their own fruits and vegetables in their gardens. Not only do they enjoy the benefits of working outside in the soil, but they also enjoy the taste of food that is grown with love, not with dollar signs in mind. Gardening is the best solution to gaining access to good food.

Part of the reason many fruits and vegetables have no taste and little nutrition is that they are picked before maturity. When tomatoes are allowed to ripen on the vine, they have a totally different full-bodied taste than when they have been picked green and ripened using artificial methods. But the main reason why these fruits and vegetables are tasteless is that they have been grown from extremely hybridized seeds.

There were once over 7,000 varieties of apples. All of these were at one time grown in orchards throughout the world. Now you will be lucky to find more than five different varieties in your local supermarket. The varieties you will find are those that have been selected by the agribusiness to be the "best" - for economical reasons, not for taste or nutrition. They produce more, will ship without bruising, can withstand higher quantities of pesticides, and produce rounder fruits that the farmer thinks can be sold more easily.

Many people have grown up in a city, and have not had the experience of growing foods in a garden. Their way of selecting fruits and vegetables are those of the market, not those of experienced gardeners. They request fruits without imperfections, such as plastic-looking fruits. They do not realize that this is not the way real fruit appears in Nature. Fruits in Nature often acquire weird shapes, have imperfections, and do not resemble fruits found in most supermarkets. They are full of flavor and vitality. The shiny, round apples in your supermarket may look great as a decoration on your table, but are tasteless in comparison to natural apples.

People need to be educated about fruits and vegetables. They need to know how to select foods not simply according to their appearance, but according to their taste and nutritional quality. Once you start eating predominantly raw fruits and vegetables, this process becomes automatic. I can tell a good avocado in a basket of inferior ones just by the way they look. I can tell if it has been sitting on the tree long enough to have its full, buttery, fatty flavor. I know what a good avocado looks like because I have been buying avocados for years, and have lived where they grow. I know what a good mango looks like, as well as a good apple. I know that when I walk into my local supermarket there is little for me to eat because none of the fruit meets my criteria of quality.

Ancient varieties of fruits and vegetables have much more taste than the varieties grown today. Tomatoes from 100-year-old seeds have an amazing taste that is sweet and powerful — nothing like a commercial tomato, even one grown by organic methods. If you plan on getting the best food possible into your body, and you are considering the idea of growing some of your own food, I suggest that you get seeds of plants that have been less hybridized. You can find sources for these ancient seeds listed at the end of this book. *Seeds of Change* in New Mexico is an excellent source for quality heirloom seeds.

Many plants have been hybridized without limit, to the point where they cannot even reproduce themselves. Seedless fruits are an example of how the methods of hybridization have been taken to an extreme. Seedless fruits have been created because of the public's demand for fruits with fewer seeds. Even though it might be more convenient to eat seedless grapes than seeded grapes, the consequences are not worth that convenience. Foods that do not have seeds have a low life-force. They cannot reproduce themselves. They have been created to be commercial products in the big business of agriculture. They often tend to contain a type of sugar that is not handled well by the body. Bananas, for example, have a tendency to raise the blood sugar too fast. The sugar in apples, on the other hand, tends to be absorbed more slowly.

I suggest that you avoid all seedless fruits. If you are unable to grow your own, try to find and purchase grapes with seeds, and watermelon with seeds. Do not go with the trend and buy these seedless abominations. Fruit needs to have seeds. This is the way they naturally grow. Humans once ate fruit and propagated the seeds, thus reproducing the fruit trees everywhere. Now this natural circle has been broken, and it cannot be without consequences. Natural laws can never be broken without consequences.

A way to incorporate more nutritious food into your diet is to eat wild foods. Wild foods have never been tampered with by modern agricultural techniques, and contain their full nutrition and taste. For example, wild dandelion, a common weed that grows almost everywhere, contains more vitamins and minerals than the best commercial fruits and vegetables grown with the use of chemical fertilizers, and sometimes on rich soil. Wild dandelion contains more vitamin C, beta-carotene, and calcium than most fruits and vegetables sold in the store. And remember that the lowly dandelion grows without any watering, fertilizers, or other care. It often grows in very poor soil, and yet has such an amazing vitality, that it takes much human effort to get rid of it. We often say, "It grows like a weed," meaning that the plant grows everywhere without any human intervention. Farmers sure would like to see their plants grow like weeds! But no, they take care of their plants, water them, feed them, and with all of this, are never able to produce a plant that has anywhere close to the nutritional quality of a wild plant. Wild plants have such an amazing life-force and vitality because they have to fight for their lives in order to survive. They have to make the best use of what little they have.

Wild fruits and vegetables grow everywhere. There are some wild fruits and vegetables that grow where you are. All you have to do to find out which plants in your area are edible is to is pick up a copy of the book, **Guide to Edible Wild Plants of North America**, and go on a hike. Asking the advice of a professional is also helpful. You can probably locate an herbalist in your area who will be happy to guide you on an edible wild plant tour.

Because of this understanding of wild foods versus hybridized foods, there are some foods that have been omitted from the recipes in this book, or used quite sparingly. Two categories of food that are not used in the **Sunfood Diet** are grains and legumes. Grains are hybridized grass seeds. At the beginning, these seeds were not edible, and contained less starch. Through time, these seeds have been cultivated and hybridized to the point that they became starchier.

The hybridized grains used in mass-produced foods come from plants that have very little life-force. If you were to take a handful of wheat berries and throw them outside of the farmer's fence, and then return six months later, what would happen? Would anything grow from these seeds? Maybe. But they would likely be weak compared to their wild counterparts. These plants only seem to survive inside of the farmer's fence, with care and watering. They have little life-force, and due to their high starch content, are not welcomed in the **Sunfood Diet**. The same thing holds true for legumes.

While it is not possible to revert entirely to wild foods, we can benefit from eating more wild foods, less hybridized foods, and by avoiding foods that are extremely hybridized, such as: grains, legumes, seedless fruits, and by growing our own food using ancient seeds.

Wild barrel cactus fruit in the Arizona desert

APPENDIX 3: ORGANIC AND COMMERCIAL FOOD

Organic food is essential for health. I feel that it is not possible, in the long term, to maintain high levels of vitality while consuming commercially grown food. Go to the local supermarket and notice how the fruits and vegetables lack vitality. If you have ever taken care of a garden, you will realize how the fruits and vegetables available in the stores do not deserve their name. They are but pale shadows of their true potential. Shiny round apples without taste. Peppers and cucumbers covered with oil. Crisp lettuce that tastes like water. Mushy, genetically-engineered tomatoes. Disappointing melons. Watery avocados. And yet still more pale-looking, weak-tasting fruits and vegetables. All of these are sprayed heavily with pesticides, herbicides, and other toxic farming chemicals. Most likely they have been grown in soil filled with chemical fertilizers, and lacking in minerals. With the great advances of modern technology, chances are that one out of four fruits or vegetables found in your supermarket has been grown on plants that were genetically manipulated.

Organic foods contain more vitamins, minerals, and other nutrients than commercial foods. They also contain fewer toxic chemicals, since they are grown without the use of chemical fertilizers and pesticides.

Studies conducted in the United States by Dr. Victor Alexander, Director of Enviro-Health Systems, have shown that 99% of humans have pesticide residues in their blood. His research for this study was conducted on 3,000 people from around the world, and showed that 99% of them carried 4 types of pesticides in their blood on average. Sometimes as many as 19.

Pesticides are toxic to health. I do not have to spend time proving that fact. Each year, many people working on farms using pesticides die of the exposure to these toxic chemicals. The presence of pesticides in our bodies is quite alarming. Although it is generally admitted that pesticides are toxic, our health officials are trying to establish a tolerance level. They are indeed trying to figure out how much of these toxic chemicals we can ingest each year without suffering from immediate health problems. To create these standards, they take into account the reality of the average American, who is of an average weight, and who consumes an average quantity of fruits and vegetables.

The reality is that the optimum level of farming chemicals on your food should be "zero." While this is difficult, if not impossible, to accomplish, you can dramatically reduce the quantity of toxic substances you ingest by consuming organically grown produce. In addition, the current organic standards do not accept the use of genetically engineered seeds and food items.

MORE MINERALS IN ORGANIC FOOD

In addition to being free of most of the toxic chemicals that commercially grown food contains, organic food contains higher levels of minerals and trace minerals, which are extremely important for our health. According to research done in France, organic produce contained, on average, 26% more minerals than commercial produce, including 56% more calcium.

The fact is that organic farmers take better care of their soil. They try to put in the soil as much as they take out, in the form of good quality compost and natural fertilizers. Most commercil farmers, on the other hand, use harsh quick-grow chemical fertilizers that do not supply the soil with a wide range of all the trace minerals that we need. The goal of the typical chemically grown farm is to grow a lot of food as fast as possible, without much concern for its quality, in terms of its nutrition.

Organic food, while being more nutritious, also tastes better. You can taste the difference. When a friend of mine came to my house one day, and had one of my organic Canadian apples. He exclaimed, "Finally, an apple that tastes like something!"

Buying organic food is supporting your future. We vote with our dollars. This is real democracy. When you go to the store, and you purchase one thing instead of something else, you are voting. You are saying, "This is what I choose. This is the type of product I wish to see around." When you purchase organic food instead of commercial food, you are voting for a better future. You are supporting the farmers who are restoring the Earth, not the ones who are destroying it. You are saying, "This is what I want. I want organic food." As the demand grows, more farmers will be interested in becoming organic farmers. If no one purchases organic food because they think it is too expensive, then there is no demand, and many farmers will go out of business. If more people purchase organic food, then it will be easier for the distributors to sell at lower prices, as they get more bulk orders. On the other hand, when you are purchasing chemically-grown food, you are voting for an industry that is poisoning you and your children and destroying the land.

So remember that next time you go shopping. Is it really about the price? Do you really think that organic food is expensive? Is it worth it to save a few dollars, at the expense of ruining your health, the health of your children, and the future of life on this planet?

GENETICALLY-ENGINEERED FOODS

Walk inside your nearest supermarket. Do you notice much difference compared to 10 years ago? Besides the look and some new products, your supermarket probably does not seem any different than it was 10 years ago. You can probably find the same types of foods and products that were available there a decade ago. But, beyond all appearances, something major has changed. You do not recognize it because it is not mentioned anywhere. No labels will let you know that about two-thirds of all the products in your supermarket now contain ingredients that have been genetically-engineered. Two out of every three products in your supermarket have been tampered with in laboratories by scientists working for big biotech corporations.

If you live in North America, purchase your fruits and vegetables at the supermarket, and want to avoid genetically-engineered foods, all we can say is, "good luck." So far, 50 genetically-engineered (GE) crops have been approved by the U.S. Department of Agriculture, including potatoes, tomatoes, melons, and beets. GE rice, wheat, cucumbers, strawberries, apples, sugarcane, and walnuts are being grown on test sites. GE foods are everywhere, and are not allowed to be labeled as such by the government. It means that the government does not want you to be able to know the difference between a conventional tomato, and a genetically-engineered tomato. Why? Because they know that if consumers had the choice, they would not buy GE foods. They want to pass GE foods under your nose without you even knowing about it.

Genetically-engineered foods are foods that have been tampered with in laboratories at the genetic level. Genetic engineering creates entirely new types of plants by altering the genetic "blueprint" of these crops. By cutting, joining, and transferring genes between unrelated species, plants are created with unique qualities. Every plant or animal is unique because of the different genes contained within the cells of that organism. Genetic engineering is the process of modifying this information, and is light years beyond typical crossbreeding. As you already know, crossbreeding is a simple technique that has been used for thousands of years to alter crops and animals. It consists of interbreeding between two varieties of the same or similar species. Genetic engineering, though, is the Frankenstein version of this theme. In crossbreeding, farmers do not stray very far between species. Two vegetables of the same family could be crossbred together, but no one would ever have considered trying to crossbreed a tomato and a fish together. Or would they? Now the barrier has been destroyed and it is possible to tamper with crops in such a radical way. The mutant tomato is a reality, and it is a quite a scary one. For example, Edinburgh scientists have mixed jellyfish genes with potatoes, resulting in spuds that glow when they need watering. The idea was to plant a few of these per hectare for water monitoring purposes, and not for human consumption. We just wonder what will happen if the potatoes get mixed in with the regular batch.

Because genetic mistakes can never be recalled, GE poses one of the greatest dangers of any technology. Genetic defects are passed on to all subsequent generations, and their effect will spread out without limit.

One of the results of GE foods is that the technology may lead to the depletion of important food elements. Genetic engineers are capable of intentionally removing or inactivateing a substance they consider undesirable in a food. The substance may have unknown but crucial qualities, such as cancer-inhibiting abilities.

GE foods that are tampered with to stay fresh longer might appear to be able to stay on the shelves for a longer period of time, but their nutritional content still decreases with every hour. And what would be the life-force of a food whose enzymes are so weak it cannot even ripen itself at a normal pace?

Since there is no labeling of GE foods, your only way to make sure that what you purchase has not been genetically engineered will be to purchase organic food exclusively, or grow your own food. Organic foods are not only more nutritious and free of the chemical fertilizers and pesticides that conventional foods contain, they are also certified to be non-genetically-engineered. They cost more than conventional foods, and might require a little effort to get, but in the end, understand that you pay now, or you pay later. There is just no other alternative.

EAT ORGANIC

Although the effect of pesticides are not felt immediately, it will not mean that they will not be felt in the long term. Many people feel that the dramatic increase in the occurrence of cancer in our society is an indication of the unforeseen damages of chemicals in our food. If you get cancer in 30 years, will you blame the commercial red bell peppers you ate all your life?

So the best insurance against this, as well as a support to the organic farming industry, is to eat as much organic food as possible starting today. When I say as much organic food as possible, I really mean: 100% by all means! Strive to eat 100% organic foods. If you cannot find organic peppers in February, well, why not just wait until next summer when they are in season again? Do you really want to eat those out-of-season peppers that have been imported from Mexico anyway, and possibly sprayed with toxic chemicals as third-world countries have less control over the amount of pesticides farmers are allowed to use? Avoid out-of-season produce. This means eating cucumbers, tomatoes, and lettuce in the summer, not in the winter. It also means eating apples in January, not the ones imported from New Zealand in July. Eating what is locally in season is also in harmony with Nature, as it is the way we are supposed to eat.

All big cities have health food stores that carry organic produce. If you have to drive an hour or so to get there, because you are living outside of the city, well, that is what you will have to do. Understand that there are not many alternatives to organic. The supermarket is not an alternative. Growing your own food is though. You can have a garden, or even grow sprouts and greens indoors. Then you get the best foods ever, 100% organic, certified by yourself!

MOST HEAVILY SPRAYED CROPS

I understand though that sometimes you will be caught somewhere with no organic food around. It happens to me sometimes. So here is a list that could be helpful.

The following crops have been found to hold high amounts of toxic residues. The research that I used is taken from the book **Diet for a Poisoned Planet** by David Steinman. Research has studied only the part of the fruits that are eaten. For example, when analyzing a cantaloupe, researchers took into consideration only the flesh of the fruit.

High-Pesticide Residue Fruits and Vegetables (in North America) include: strawberries, cantaloupes (from Mexico), apples, pears, spinach, raisins, grapes, peppers, cucumbers, peanuts, celery.

The following crops are relatively safe. They are our choices when organically grown foods are not available. Remember that this does not guarantee that they will not be genetically-engineered, but at the year of publication (2001), these foods should not be. Remember that most of these items still contained pesticide residues, but in much smaller quantities than in the other foods analyzed.

Relatively Safe Fruits & Vegetables (in North America) include: papayas, watermelons, citrus (except tangerines), corn, cabbage, all nuts except peanuts.

A last point: some people complain that organic food is too expensive and that they cannot afford it, since they have a low income and a large family to feed. My answer is that you either pay now, or you will pay later. Look at it this way: how much will it cost when you and your children suffer from the long-term effects of pesticide poisoning? With the introduction of these genetically-engineered foods, how much will it cost you to face the now-unknown long-term effects resulting from the consumption of such foods? How much is that worth? Is that worth the price? Do you really save anything in the end when you are encouraging an industry that destroys our precious planet?

We have to realize that as more people start eating organic foods, it will become more affordable and more available. The organic food industry is a blossoming industry currently growing at the rate of 20% per year. It is very exciting to be part of a movement that is working toward bringing back real food onto our tables.

As a last word to conclude this work. I would like to thank all of you who invested money to buy this book, and invested your time to learn to eat better. I hope you had as much fun reading this book as I had writing it, and that by now you understand the basic concept behind it: *to be alive, eat alive!*

ARTIST COMMENTS

Sara Honeycutt is the artist for **The Sunfood Cuisine**.

"An epiphany or two occurred for me while creating the artwork for this book. The similarities between the intricate patterns found both in nature and in our bodies became startlingly obvious while drawing the veins of a beet leaf, the juice-cells of an orange slice, the brain-like folds of a sliced cabbage, the inner seed caverns of an apple and a fig, and the seeds of a tomato gathered to the central pulp like an image of nursing kittens.

While discussing this with John McCabe, the editor for **The Sunfood Cuisine**, I learned that this is the very reason why living foods are so healthful to the body. The patterns of uncooked living plants, and especially their intact cellular and energetic activity, match those found in the physical bodies and living cells of animals and humans. When we eat plants, these natural patterns are taken into the cells of our bodies and become part of us — food at its deepest level.

Being able to actually 'see' this has left a profound impression, and has revealed to me a much deeper relationship between living plants and the human body. I am glad to have been able to create the artwork and reflect this vision for those enjoying this book."

—Sara Honeycutt

Thanks to the editor John McCabe, the graphic designer Lyn Bradley, author Frédéric Patenaude, publisher David Wolfe, and my companion Riksharaj, for their incredible work and vital support.

Sara Honeycutt resides in California. She can be reached by email at: **sarahoneycutt@earthlink.net**, and her artwork and book cover illustrations may be viewed by accessing: **http://home.earthlink.net/~sarahoneycutt**

Products mentioned in **The Sunfood Cuisine**
available for purchase through www.rawfood.com
(see order form for instructions on placing an order)

Book: "**The Sunfood Cuisine**" by Frédéric Patenaude
Book: "**Sunfood Diet Success System, The**" by David Wolfe
Book: "**Eating For Beauty**" by David Wolfe
Book: "**Fit For Life I & II**" by Harvey & Marilyn Diamond
Book: "**Don't Drink Your Milk**" by Frank A. Oski
Book: "**Diet For A New America**" by John Robbins
Book: "**Field Guide To Edible Wild Plants**" by Bradford Angler
Book: "**Raw-Food Treatment Of Cancer**" by Kristina Nolfi
Blender: "**Vita-Mix Blender with variable speed**"
Nutcracker: "**Krakanut —World's Finest Nutcracker**"
Dehydrator: "**Excalibur 5-tray**" (Model ED-2500)
Dehydrator: "**Excalibur 9-tray**" (Model ED-2900)
Dehydrator Accessory: "**Teflex Sheet**"
Seed Grinder: "**Flax Seed Grinder**"
Organic Food: "**Olives: Greek, Kalmata, Italian, Moroccan, Peruvian**"
Organic Food: "**Raw, Organic Stone-Pressed Extra Virgin Olive Oil**"
Organic Food: "**Raw, Organic, in-the-shell, Nuts: Macadamias , Almonds,
   Hazelnuts, Pecans, Pistachios, Walnuts**"
Organic Food: "**Raw, Organic, out-of-the-shell, Brazil Nuts and Pecans**"
Organic Food: "**Raw Wild Unheated Cashews with and without skins**"
Organic Food: "**Dried Fruit: Apricots, Calimyrna Figs, Black Mission
   Figs, Mangos, Raisins**"
Organic Food: "**Celtic Grey Minerals: Sea Salt**"
Organic Food: "**Natures First Law: Coconut Butter**"
Organic Food: "**Raw, Organic: Almond Butter, Pumpkin Seed Butter, and
   Sunflower Seed Butter**"
Soy Sauce: "**Raw, Unpasteurized-Nama Shoyu**"
Food Processor: "**Saladacco Spiralizer**"
Juicer: "**Champion Juicer-Commerical Model**"
Juicer: "**Green Power Juicer**"
Juicer: "**Green Life Juice Extractor**"

APPENDIX 4: RESOURCES

IMPORTANT RAW-VEGAN WEBSITES

The Raw Vegan Diet
www.rawvegan.com

Nature's First Law
www.rawfood.com

David Wolfe
www.davidwolfe.com

Nature's First Law Inc.
www.rawfood.com
Your #1 Source For All Raw-Vegan Lifestyle Products
PO Box 900202
San Diego, CA 92190 USA
Email: nature@rawfood.com
1-888-RAW-FOOD OR 619-596-7979
Fax: 619-596-7997
International +001-619-596-7979

HEIRLOOM SEED RESOURCE

Seeds Of Change
PO Box 15700
Santa Fe, NM 87506-5700
1-888-762-7333
505-438-8080
Fax: 505-438-7052
www.seedsofchange.com

UNIQUE PRODUCT RESOURCE
First Choice Nutritionals
PO Box 2823
Sequim, WA 98382
www.1stchoicenutritionals.com
1stchoice@prodigy.net
1-888-357-3456

This company distributes unique holistic products.

Just Eat An Apple

Magazine
(4 issues/year)
50+ pages
To order online: www.rawfood.com

Would you like to learn more about the raw-vegan diet? Would you like to meet other raw-vegans, learn new recipes, and stay updated as to what's happening in the raw-food world?

Subscribe to "**Just Eat An Apple**" magazine!

"Just Eat An Apple" is the foremost magazine on the raw-vegan diet. It includes regular articles on various raw-food and vegan issues, such as health, ecology, and organic farming. Raw-food recipes are included in each issue, as well as letters to the editor, a question and answer column, and articles written by a wide variety of experts. It is also the networking magazine of the raw-vegan community, and the place to connect with other raw-foodists. It contains updated information on what is happening in the raw-vegan scene. "Just Eat An Apple" has subscribers in over 38 countries. Stay updated, learn more about this — subscribe today!

To subscribe to "Just Eat An Apple," send a check or money order, made out to **Nature's First Law**, along with your address.

Nature's First Law
Just Eat An Apple Department
PO Box 900202
San Diego, CA 92190
U.S.A.

The rates are the following:

USA & Canada
-One year (4 issues) US$24
-Two years (8 issues) is $42

All other countries
US $35 for one year (4 issues)
US $58 for two years (8 issues)

BIBLIOGRAPHY

Alexander, Joe, **Blatant Raw-Foodist Propaganda**, (Blue Dolphin, 1990).
Arlin, Dini, Wolfe, **Nature's First Law: the Raw-Food Diet** (Maul Bros., 1999).
Arlin, Stephen, **Raw Power**, (Maul Bros., 1998).
Burger, Guy Claude, **Instinctothérapie: Manger Vrai** (Édition du Rocher, 1990).
Cousens, Dr. Gabriel, **Conscious Eating** (North Atlantic Books, 2nd Edition).
Diamond, Harvey & Marilyn, **Fit For Life**, (Mass Market Paperback, 1987).
Esser, William L, **Dictionary of Natural Foods**, (Natural Hygiene Press, 1983).
Gagnon, Yves, **La culture écologique** (Éditions Colloïdales, 1984).
Howell, Dr. Edward, **Enzyme Nutrition: the Food Enzymes Concept**, (Avery
    Publishing Group, 1986).
Kulvinskas, Viktoras, **Survival into the 21st Century**, (21st Century Publication,
    1993).
Marcus, Erik, **Vegan: the New Ethics of Eating**, (Mc Books Press, 1998).
Meyerowitz, Steve, **Sprouts: the Miracle Food**, (Sproutman Publications, 1999).
Onstad, Dianne, **Whole Foods Companion**, (Chelsea Green, 1996).
Safron, Jeremy; Underkoffer, Renée, **The Raw Truth: the Art of Loving Foods** (Raw
    Truth Press, 1997).
Shelton, Herbet, **Food Combining Made Easy** (Willow Publishing, 1940).
Steinman, David, **Diet for a Poisoned Planet**, (Harmony Books, 1990).
Wigmore, Ann, **The Sprouting Book**, (Avery Publishing Group, 1986).
Wolfe, David, **The Sunfood Diet Success System**, (Maul Bros., 2000).
Wolfe, David, **Eating For Beauty**, (Maul Bros. 2002).

Contact the Author
If you desire to invite the author of this book to do a raw-food demonstration
class in your city, interview him for the press, or for any other queries or
comments on this book, you can e-mail him directly.
Email: frederic@rawvegan.com

To keep in touch with what is going on in the raw-vegan world, please visit the
following websites regularly:
http://**www.rawfood.com**
http://**www.rawvegan.com**

A

H

I

O

okra, 62

olive, 26, 56, 68, 100-2, 115, 118-21, 124, 126-9, 135-40, 143, 145, 184-6, 191, 193, 194, 198, 200-8, 214, 220, 221

olive cream, 193

olive oil, 26, 68, 101, 121, 126, 138

onions, 82, 116, 125, 137, 190, 194, 199

orange, 46, 124, 125, 152, 158, 163, 164

orange juice, 47, 48, 109, 123, 128, 158, 161, 163, 165, 172, 177, 179, 191, 193, 198, 199

orange milk, 158

orange-avo, 164

orange-grapefruit, 152

oregano, 96-9, 125, 126, 129, 139, 141, 143, 191, 201, 202, 207, 210, 211

organic & commercial food, 229

organically grown, 19, 33, 38, 52, 62, 87, 229, 233

oski, dr. frank, 155

oxalic acid, 50, 63, 78, 83

P

pad thai, 199

papaya, 16, 24, 47, 72, 161, 163, 169, 178, 233

papaya-orange, 163

paprika, 96, 98, 126, 130

parsley, 78, 96, 98, 115, 118, 119, 127, 129, 134, 136-8, 140-9, 185, 187, 193, 198, 200, 203, 221

parsley dressing, 127

passion fruit, 47

passion fruit juice, 115, 116, 124, 125

pasta al frederico, 201

pasta marinara, 201

pâté d'italie, 187

pâté de chez-nous, 187

patenada, 194

pâtés, 77, 84, 87, 88, 91, 92, 93, 107, 108, 183-187, 189, 209

Q

R

S

OPTIONS FOR ORDERING FROM NATURE'S FIRST LAW:

1. **Fill out order form and mail to**:

> Nature's First Law Inc.
> P.O. Box 900202
> San Diego, CA 92190

2. **Order by Phone:**

> (888) RAW-FOOD or (619) 596-7979 / Int'l: +001-619-596-7979

3. **Order by Email**: order@rawfood.com

4. **Order via our secure, encrypted Internet Superstore**:

> www.rawfood.com

> ## Shipping & Handling:

United States:
Priority Mail (1-3 days): $4.50 for 1 item (oversized and glass items are extra), $1.50 for each additional item. UPS (1-7 days) available for orders over four pounds. Rates vary depending on weight and shipping zone.
> **California Residents add sales tax: 7.75%**

Canada & Mexico:
*Air Mail: $8.00 for 1 item, $2.00 for each additional item.
Outside North America:
*Air Mail: $10.00 for 1 item, $6.00 for each additional item. Surface mail shipping is also available.
Australia & New Zealand:
*Air Mail: $12.00 for 1 item, $6.00 for each additional item. Surface mail shipping is also available.

Checks & Money Orders:
All checks and money orders must be in US Dollars and payable to:
> Nature's First Law.
We accept International money orders in US Dollars, drawn on a US bank.

Credit Cards:
We accept Visa, Mastercard, Discover, & American Express.
Be sure to include the Expiration Date.

*Indicates book shipping only, for all other product orders please call for a shipping & handling estimate. Shipping is automatically calculated as you order from rawfood.com

Nature's First Law - Product Order Form

Order Date: ___/___/___   Please Print Clearly

Ship To: *Bill To: (if different than "ship to")*

Name:_____   Name:_____

Address:_____   Address:_____

City: _____   City: _____

State: _____ Zip Code: _____   State: _____ Zip Code: _____

Country: _____   Country: _____

Phone Number: _____   Phone Number: _____

Email Address: _____   Email Address: _____

Item Description	Quantity	Item Price	Total Price

Credit Card Orders (Circle one): Visa, Mastercard, Discover, American Express   **Sub Total** |_____

Credit Card #: ____/____/____/____ exp.   CA Sales Tax (7.75%) |_____

Signature: _____   ****Shipping & Handling** |_____

**See Shipping & Handling Charges   Total |_____

All Checks Made Payable to: Nature's First Law

PO Box 900202, San Diego, CA 92190 USA
1-888-RAW-FOOD OR 619-596-7979
Fax: 619-596-7997, International +001-619-596-7979
Internet: www.rawfood.com
Email: order@rawfood.com